A CHILD'S BOOK OF
SAINTS

WILLIAM CANTON

1st WORLD LIBRARY
Literary Society

A Child's Book of Saints

William Canton

© 1st World Library, 2009
PO Box 2211
Fairfield, IA 52556
www.1stworldlibrary.com
First Edition

LCCN: 2009923513

Softcover ISBN: 978-1-4218-8891-0
Hardcover ISBN: 978-1-4218-8990-0
eBook ISBN: 978-1-4218-8792-0

Purchase *"A Child's Book of Saints"*
as a traditional bound book at:
www.1stWorldLibrary.com/purchase.asp?ISBN=978-1-4218-8891-0

1st World Library is a literary, educational organization
dedicated to:

- Creating a free internet library of downloadable ebooks

- Hosting writing competitions and offering book publishing
scholarships.

Interested in more 1st World Library books? contact:
literacy@1stworldlibrary.com
Check us out at: www.1stworldlibrary.com

1st World Library Literary Society

Giving Back to the World

"If you want to work on the core problem, it's early school literacy."

- James Barksdale, former CEO of Netscape

"No skill is more crucial to the future of a child, or to a democratic and prosperous society, than literacy."

- Los Angeles Times

"Literacy... means far more than learning how to read and write... The aim is to transmit... knowledge and promote social participation."

- UNESCO

"Literacy is not a luxury, it is a right and a responsibility. If our world is to meet the challenges of the twenty-first century we must harness the energy and creativity of all our citizens."

- President Bill Clinton

"Parents should be encouraged to read to their children, and teachers should be equipped with all available techniques for teaching literacy, so the varying needs and capacities of individual kids can be taken into account."

- Hugh Mackay

This is fairy gold, boy;
And I will prove it so.

—Shakespeare

Every man I will go with thee, be thy guide
in thy most need to go by thy side.

EDITOR'S NOTE

"A Child's Book of Saints" was first published in 1898, when Mr. Canton had already found his audience. The book is a near successor indeed to his "W. V.: Her Book," and to "The Invisible Playmate"; and W. V. again acts as guardian elf and guide to this new region of the child's earthly paradise. The Saints are here treated with a simplicity that is almost or altogether childlike, and with an unforced imagination which is only to be learnt by becoming as a child. And this is perhaps why, although comparatively a new book, it has the air of something pleasantly old, and written long ago; and thus wins its way into the children's library of old favourite authors.

Mr. Canton's published works, up to January 1906, comprise:—"A Lost Epic, and other Poems," 1887. "The Invisible Playmate: a Story of the Unseen," 1894, 1897. "W. V., Her Book and Various Verses," 1896. "A Child's Book of Saints," 1898, 1902. "Children's Sayings, Edited, with a Digression on the Small People," 1900. "The True Annals of Fairyland" (The Reign of King Herla), 1900, &c. "In Memory of W. V." (Winifred Vida Canton), 1901. "The Comrades: Poems, Old and New," 1902. "What is the Bible Society?" 1903. "The Story of the Bible Society," 1904. "A History of the British and Foreign Bible Society," 1904. "Little Hands and God's Book: a Sketch of the Bible Society," 1804-1904, 1905.

CONTENTS

A saint, whose very name I have forgotten, had a vision, in which he saw Satan standing before the throne of God; and, listening, he heard the evil spirit say, "Why hast Thou condemned me, who have offended Thee but once, whilst Thou savest thousands of men who have offended Thee many times?" God answered him, "Hast thou once asked pardon of me?"

Behold the Christian mythology! It is the dramatic truth, which has its worth and effect independently of the literal truth, and which even gains nothing by being fact. What matter whether the saint had or had not heard the sublime words which I have just quoted! The great point is to know that pardon is refused only to him who does not ask it.

COUNT DE MAISTRE.

IN THE FOREST OF STONE

Looking down the vista of trees and houses from the slope of our garden, W. V. saw the roof and spire of the church of the Oak-men showing well above the green huddle of the Forest.

"It is a pretty big church, isn't it, father?" she asked, as she pointed it out to me.

It was a most picturesque old-fashioned church, though in my thoughtlessness I had mistaken it for a beech and a tall poplar growing apparently side by side; but the moment she spoke I perceived my illusion.

"I expect, if we were anywhere about on a Sunday morning," she surmised, with a laugh, "we should see hundreds and hundreds of Oak-girls and Oak-boys going in schools to service."

"Dressed in green silk, with bronze boots and pink feathers—the colours of the new oak-leaves, eh?"

"Oh, father, it would be lovely!" in a burst of ecstasy. "Oughtn't we to go and find the way to their church?"

We might do something much less amusing. Accordingly we took the bearings of the green spire with the skill of veteran explorers. It lay due north, so that if we travelled by the way of the North Star we should be certain to find it. Wheeling the Man before us, we made a North Star track for ourselves through the underwood and over last year's rustling beech-leaves, till Guy ceased babbling and crooning, and dropped into a slumber, as he soon does in the fresh of the morning. Then we had to go slowly for fear he should be wakened by the noise of the dead wood underfoot, for, as we passed over it with wheels and boots, it snapped and crackled like a freshly-kindled fire. It was a relief to get at last to the soft matting of brown needles and cones under the Needle-trees, for there we could go pretty quickly without either jolting him or making a racket.

We went as far as we were able that day, and we searched in glade and lawn, in coppice and dingle, but never a trace could we find of the sylvan minster where the Oak-people worship. As we wandered through the Forest we came upon a number of notice boards nailed high up on the trunks of various trees, but when W. V. discovered that these only repeated the same stern legend: "Caution. Persons breaking, climbing upon, or otherwise damaging," she indignantly resented this incessant intrusion on the innocent enjoyment of free foresters. How much nicer it would have been if there had been a hand on one of these repressive boards, with the inscription: "This way to the North Star Church;" or, if a caution was really necessary for some of the people who entered the Forest, to say: "The public are requested not to disturb the Elves, Birch-ladies, and Oak-men;" but of course the most delightful thing would be to have a different fairy-tale written up in clear letters on each of the boards, and a seat close by where one could rest and read it comfortably.

I told her there were several forests I had explored, in which something like that was really done; only the stories were not fairy-tales, but legends of holy men and women; and among

William Canton

the branches of the trees were fixed most beautifully coloured glass pictures of those holy people, who had all lived and died, and some of whom had been buried, in those forests, hundreds of years ago. Most of the forests were very ancient—older than the thrones of many kingdoms; and men lived and delighted in them long before Columbus sailed into unknown seas to discover America. Many, indeed, had been blown down and destroyed by a terrible storm which swept over the world when Henry VIII. ruled in England, and only wrecks of them now remained for any one to see, but others, which had survived the wild weather of those days, were as wonderful and as lovely as a dream. The tall trees in them sent out curving branches which interlaced high overhead, shutting out the blue sky and making a sweet and solemn dimness, and nearly all the light that streamed in between the fair round trunks and the arching boughs was like that of a splendid sunset, only it was there all day long and never faded out till night fell. And in some of the forests there were great magical roses, of a hundred brilliant colours crowded together, and as big as the biggest cart-wheel, or bigger.

These woods were places of happy quietude and comfort and gladness of heart; but, instead of Oak-men, there were many Angels.

Here and there, too, in the silent avenues, mighty warriors and saintly abbots, and statesmen bishops, and it might be even a king or a queen, had been buried; and over their graves there were sometimes images of them lying carved in marble or alabaster, and sometimes there had been built the loveliest little chapels all sculptured over with tracery of flowers and foliage.

"True, father?"

"True as true, dear. Some day I shall take you to see

for yourself."

We know a dip in a dingle where the woodcutters have left a log among the hazels, and here, having wheeled Guy into a dappling of sunny discs and leaf-shadows in a grassy bay, we sat down on the log, and talked in an undertone. Our failure to find the Oak-men's church reminded me of the old legends of lost and invisible churches, the bells of which are heard ringing under the snow, or in the depths of the woods, or far away in burning deserts, or fathom-deep beneath the blue sea; but the pilgrim or the chance wayfarer who has heard the music of the bells has never succeeded in discovering the way that leads to the lost church. It is on the clear night of St. John's Day, the longest day of the year, or on the last hour of Christmas Eve, that these bells are heard pealing most sweet and clear.

It was in this way that we came to tell Christian legends and to talk of saints and hermits, of old abbeys and minsters, of visions and miracles and the ministry of Angels. Guy, W. V. thought, might be able, if only he could speak, to tell us much about heaven and the Angels; it was so short a time since he left them. She herself had quite forgotten, but, then—deprecatingly—it was so long and long and long ago; "eight years, a long time for me."

The faith and the strange vivid daydreams of the Middle Ages were a new world into which she was being led along enchanted footpaths; quite different from the worldly world of the "Old Romans," and of English history; more real it seemed and more credible, for all its wonders, than the world of elves and water-maidens. Delightful as it was, it was scarce believable that fairies ever carried a little girl up above the tree-tops and swung her in the air from one to another; but when St. Catherine of Siena was a little child, and went to be a hermit in the woods, and got terribly frightened, and lost her way, and sat down to cry, the Angels, you know, did really and truly waft her up on their wings and carried her to the valley of Fontebranda, which was very near home. And when she was quite a little thing and used to say her prayers going up to bed, the Angels would come to her and just "whip" her right up the stairs in an instant!

Occasionally these legends brought us to the awful brink of religious controversies and insoluble mysteries, but, like those gentle savages who honour the water-spirits by hanging garlands from tree to tree across the river, W. V. could always fling a bridge of flowers over our abysses. "Our sense," she would declare, "is nothing to God's; and though big people have more sense than children, the sense of all the big people in the world put together would be no sense to His." "We are only little babies to Him; we do not understand Him at all." Nothing seemed clearer to her than the reasonableness of one legend which taught that though God always answers our prayers, He does not always answer in the way we would like, but in some better way than we know. "Yes," she observed, "He is just a dear old Father." Anything about our Lord engrossed her imagination; and it was a frequent wish of hers that He would come again. "Then,"—poor perplexed little mortal! whose difficulties one could not even guess at—"we should be quite sure of things. Miss Catherine tells us from books: He would tell us from His memory. People would not be so cruel to Him now. Queen Victoria would not allow any one to crucify Him."

I don't think that W. V., in spite of her confidence in my good faith, was quite convinced of the existence of those old forests of which I had told her, until I explained that they were forests of stone, which, if men did not mar them, would blossom for centuries unchanged, though the hands that planted them had long been blown in dust about the world. She understood all that I meant when we visited York and

Westminster, and walked through the long avenues of stone palms and pines, with their overarching boughs, and gazed at the marvellous rose-windows in which all the jewels of the world seemed to have been set, and saw the colours streaming through the gorgeous lancets and high many-lighted casements. After that it was delightful to turn over engravings and photographs of ruined abbeys and famous old churches at home and abroad, and to anticipate the good time when we should visit them together, and perhaps not only descend into the crypts but go through the curious galleries which extend over the pillars of the nave, and even climb up to the leaded roof of the tower, or dare the long windy staircases and ladders which mount into the spire, and so look down on the quaint map of streets, and houses, and gardens, and squares, hundreds of feet below.

She liked to hear how some of those miracles of stone had been fashioned and completed—how monks in the days of old had travelled over the land with the relics of saints, collecting treasure of all sorts for the expense of the work; how sometimes the people came in hundreds dragging great oaks and loads of quarried stone, and bringing fat hogs, beans, corn, and beer for the builders and their workmen; how even queens carried block or beam to the masons, so that with their own hands they might help in the glorious labour; and poor old women gave assistance by cooking food and washing and spinning and weaving and making and mending; how when the foundations were blessed kings and princes and powerful barons laid each a stone, and when the choir sang the antiphon, "And the foundations of the wall were garnished with all manner of precious stones," they threw costly rings and jewels and chains of gold into the trench; and how years and generations passed away, and abbots and bishops and architects and masons and sculptors and labourers died, but new men took their places, and still the vast work went on, and the beautiful pile rose higher and

William Canton

higher into the everlasting heavens.

Then, too, we looked back at the vanished times when the world was all so different from our world of to-day; and in green and fruitful spots among the hills and on warm river-lawns and in olden cities of narrow streets and overhanging roofs, there were countless abbeys and priories and convents; and thousands of men and women lived the life of prayer and praise and austerity and miracle and vision which is described in the legends of the Saints. We lingered in the pillared cloisters where the black-letter chronicles were written in Latin, and music was scored and hymns were composed, and many a rare manuscript was illuminated in crimson and blue and emerald and gold; and we looked through the fair arches into the cloister-garth where in the green sward a grave lay ever ready to receive the remains of the next brother who should pass away from this little earth to the glory of Paradise. What struck W. V. perhaps most of all was, that in some leafy places these holy houses were so ancient that even the blackbirds and throstles had learned to repeat some of the cadences of the church music, and in those places the birds still continue to pipe them, though nothing now remains of church or monastery except the name of some field or street or well, which people continue to use out of old habit and custom.

It was with the thought of helping the busy little brain to realise something of that bygone existence, with its strange modes of thought, its unquestioning faith in the unseen and eternal, its vivid consciousness of the veiled but constant presence of the holy and omnipotent God, its stern self-repression and its tender charity, its lovely ideals and haunting legends, that I told W. V. the stories in this little book. It mattered little to her or to me that that existence had its dark shadows contrasting with its celestial light: it was the light that concerned us, not the shadows.

Some of the stories were told on the log, while Guy slept in his mail-cart in the dappled shelter of the dingle; others by a winter fire when the days were short, and the cry of the wind in the dark made it easy for one to believe in wolves; others in the Surrey hills, a year ago, in a sandy hollow crowned with bloom of the ling, and famous for a little pool where the martins alight to drink and star the mud with a maze of claw-tracks; and yet again, others, this year,[1] under the dry roof of the pines of Anstiebury, when the fosse of the old Briton settlement was dripping with wet, and the woods were dim with the smoke of rain, and the paths were red with the fallen bloom of the red chestnuts and white with the flourish of May and brown with the catkins of the oak, and the cuckoo, calling in Mosses Wood, was answered from Redlands and the Warren, and the pines where we sat (snug and dry) looked so solemn and dark that, with a little fancy, it was easy to change the living greenwood into the forest of stone.

As they were told, under the pressure of an insatiable listener, so have they been written, save for such a phrase, here and there, as slips more readily from the pen than from the tongue.

Of the stories which were told, but which have not been written for this book, if W. V. should question me, I shall answer in the wise words of the Greybeard of Broce-Liande: "However hot thy thirst, and however pleasant to assuage it, leave clear water in the well."

[1] The year of the happy hills, 1898.

THE SONG OF THE MINSTER

When John of Fulda became Prior of Hethholme, says the old chronicle, he brought with him to the Abbey many rare and costly books—beautiful illuminated missals and psalters and portions of the Old and New Testament. And he presented rich vestments to the Minster; albs of fine linen, and copes embroidered with flowers of gold. In the west front he built two great arched windows filled with marvellous storied glass. The shrine of St. Egwin he repaired at vast outlay, adorning it with garlands in gold and silver, but the colour of the flowers was in coloured gems, and in like fashion the little birds in the nooks of the foliage. Stalls and benches of carved oak he placed in the choir; and many other noble works he had wrought in his zeal for the glory of God's house.

In all the western land was there no more fair or stately Minster than this of the Black Monks, with the peaceful township on one side, and on the other the sweet meadows and the acres of wheat and barley sloping down to the slow river, and beyond the river the clearings in the ancient forest.

But Thomas the Sub-prior was grieved and troubled in his mind by the richness and the beauty of all he saw about him, and by the Prior's eagerness to be ever adding some new work in stone, or oak, or metal, or jewels.

"Surely," he said to himself, "these things are unprofitable—
less to the honour of God than to the pleasure of the eye and
the pride of life and the luxury of our house! Had so much
treasure not been wasted on these vanities of bright colour
and carved stone, our dole to the poor of Christ might have
been fourfold, and they filled with good things. But now let
our almoner do what best he may, I doubt not many a leper
sleeps cold, and many a poor man goes lean with hunger."

This the Sub-prior said, not because his heart was quick with
fellowship for the poor, but because he was of a narrow and
gloomy and grudging nature, and he could conceive of no
true service of God which was not one of fasting and praying, of fear and trembling, of joylessness and mortification.

Now you must know that the greatest of the monks and the
hermits and the holy men were not of this kind. In their love
of God they were blithe of heart, and filled with a rare
sweetness and tranquillity of soul, and they looked on the
goodly earth with deep joy, and they had a tender care for the
wild creatures of wood and water. But Thomas had yet much
to learn of the beauty of holiness.

Often in the bleak dark hours of the night he would leave his
cell and steal into the Minster, to fling himself on the cold
stones before the high altar; and there he would remain,
shivering and praying, till his strength failed him.

It happened one winter night, when the thoughts I have
spoken of had grown very bitter in his mind, Thomas guided
his steps by the glimmer of the sanctuary lamp to his
accustomed place in the choir. Falling on his knees, he laid
himself on his face with the palms of his outstretched hands
flat on the icy pavement. And as he lay there, taking a cruel
joy in the freezing cold and the torture of his body, he
became gradually aware of a sound of far-away yet most

heavenly music.

He raised himself to his knees to listen, and to his amazement he perceived that the whole Minster was pervaded by a faint mysterious light, which was every instant growing brighter and clearer. And as the light increased the music grew louder and sweeter, and he knew that it was within the sacred walls. But it was no mortal minstrelsy.

The strains he heard were the minglings of angelic instruments, and the cadences of voices of unearthly loveliness. They seemed to proceed from the choir about him, and from the nave and transept and aisles; from the pictured windows and from the clerestory and from the vaulted roofs. Under his knees he felt that the crypt was throbbing and droning like a huge organ.

Sometimes the song came from one part of the Minster, and then all the rest of the vast building was silent; then the music was taken up, as it were in response, in another part; and yet again voices and instruments would blend in one indescribable volume of harmony, which made the huge pile thrill and vibrate from roof to pavement.

As Thomas listened, his eyes became accustomed to the celestial light which encompassed him, and he saw—he could scarce credit his senses that he saw—the little carved angels of the oak stalls in the choir clashing their cymbals and playing their psalteries.

He rose to his feet, bewildered and half terrified. At that moment the mighty roll of unison ceased, and from many parts of the church there came a concord of clear high voices, like a warbling of silver trumpets, and Thomas heard the words they sang. And the words were these—

Tibi omnes Angeli.
To Thee all Angels cry aloud.

So close to him were two of these voices that Thomas looked up to the spandrels in the choir, and he saw that it was the carved angels leaning out of the spandrels that were singing. And as they sang the breath came from their stone lips white and vaporous into the frosty air.

He trembled with awe and astonishment, but the wonder of what was happening drew him towards the altar. The beauty-ful tabernacle work of the altar screen contained a double range of niches filled with the statues of saints and kings; and these, he saw, were singing. He passed slowly onward with his arms outstretched, like a blind man who does not know the way he is treading.

The figures on the painted glass of the lancets were singing.

The winged heads of the baby angels over the marble memorial slabs were singing.

The lions and griffons and mythical beasts of the finials were singing.

The effigies of dead abbots and priors were singing on their tombs in bay and chantry.

The figures in the frescoes on the walls were singing.

On the painted ceiling westward of the tower the verses of the Te Deum, inscribed in letters of gold above the shields of kings and princes and barons, were visible in the divine light, and the very words of these verses were singing, like living things.

And the breath of all these as they sang turned to a smoke as of incense in the wintry air, and floated about the high pillars of the Minster.

Suddenly the music ceased, all save the deep organ-drone.

Then Thomas heard the marvellous antiphon repeated in the bitter darkness outside; and that music, he knew, must be the response of the galleries of stone kings and queens, of abbots and virgin martyrs, over the western portals, and of the monstrous gargoyles along the eaves.

When the music ceased in the outer darkness, it was taken up again in the interior of the Minster.

At last there came one stupendous united cry of all the singers, and in that cry even the organ-drone of the crypt, and the clamour of the brute stones of pavement and pillar, of wall and roof, broke into words articulate. And the words were these:

Per singulos dies, benedicimus Te.
Day by day: we magnify Thee,
And we worship Thy name: ever world without end.

As the wind of the summer changes into the sorrowful wail of the yellowing woods, so the strains of joyous worship changed into a wail of supplication; and as he caught the words, Thomas too raised his voice in wild entreaty:

Miserere nostri, Domine, miserere nostri.
O Lord, have mercy upon us: have mercy upon us.

And then his senses failed him, and he sank to the ground in a long swoon.

When he came to himself all was still, and all was dark save for the little yellow flower of light in the sanctuary lamp.

As he crept back to his cell he saw with unsealed eyes how churlishly he had grudged God the glory of man's genius and the service of His dumb creatures, the metal of the hills, and the stone of the quarry, and the timber of the forest; for now he knew that at all seasons, and whether men heard the music or not, the ear of God was filled by day and by night with an everlasting song from each stone of the vast Minster:

We magnify Thee,
And we worship Thy name: ever world without end.

William Canton

THE PILGRIM OF A NIGHT

In the ancient days of faith the doors of the churches used to be opened with the first glimmer of the dawn in summer, and long before the moon had set in winter; and many a ditcher and woodcutter and ploughman on his way to work used to enter and say a short prayer before beginning the labour of the long day.

Now it happened that in Spain there was a farm-labourer named Isidore, who went daily to his early prayer, whatever the weather might be. His fellow-workmen were slothful and careless, and they gibed and jeered at his piety, but when they found that their mockery had no effect upon him, they spoke spitefully of him in the hearing of the master, and accused him of wasting in prayer the time which he should have given to his work.

When the farmer heard of this he was displeased, and he spoke to Isidore and bade him remember that true and faithful service was better than any prayer that could be uttered in words.

"Master," replied Isidore, "what you say is true, but it is also true that no time is ever lost in prayer. Those who pray have God to work with them, and the ploughshare which He guides draws as goodly and fruitful a furrow as another."

This the master could not deny, but he resolved to keep a watch on Isidore's comings and goings, and early on the morrow he went to the fields.

In the sharp air of the autumn morning he saw this one and that one of his men sullenly following the plough behind the oxen, and taking little joy in the work. Then, as he passed on to the rising ground, he heard a lark carolling gaily in the grey sky, and in the hundred-acre where Isidore was engaged he saw to his amazement not one plough but three turning the hoary stubble into ruddy furrows. And one plough was drawn by oxen and guided by Isidore, but the two others were drawn and guided by Angels of heaven.

When next the master spoke to Isidore it was not to reproach him, but to beg that he might be remembered in his prayers.

Now the one great longing of Isidore's life was to visit that hallowed and happy country beyond the sea in which our Lord lived and died for us. He longed to gaze on the fields in which the Shepherds heard the song of the Angels, and to know each spot named in the Gospels. All that he could save from his earnings Isidore hoarded up, so that one day, before he was old, he might set out on pilgrimage to the Holy Land. It took many years to swell the leather bag in which he kept his treasure; and each coin told of some pleasure, or comfort, or necessary which he had denied himself.

Now, when at length the bag was grown heavy, and it began to appear not impossible that he might yet have his heart's desire, there came to his door an aged pilgrim with staff and scallop-shell, who craved food and shelter for the night. Isidore bade him welcome, and gave him such homely fare as he might—bread and apples and cheese and thin wine, and satisfied his hunger and thirst.

　　　　　William Canton

Long they talked together of the holy places and of the joy of treading the sacred dust that had borne the marks of the feet of Christ. Then the pilgrim spoke of the long and weary journey he had yet to go, begging his way from village to village (for his scrip was empty) till he could prevail on some good mariner to give him ship-room and carry him to the green isle of home, far away on the edge of sunset. Thinking of those whom he had left and who might be dead before he could return, the pilgrim wept, and his tears so moved the heart of Isidore that he brought forth his treasure and said:

"This have I saved in the great hope that one day I might set eyes on what thou hast beheld, and sit on the shores of the Lake of Galilee, and gaze on the hill of Calvary. But thy need is very great. Take it, and hasten home (ere they be dead) to those who love thee and look for thy coming; and if thou findest them alive bid them pray for me."

And when they had prayed together Isidore and the pilgrim lay down to sleep.

In the first sweet hours of the restful night Isidore became aware that he was walking among strange fields on a hillside, and on the top of a hill some distance away there were the white walls and low flat-roofed houses of a little town; and some one was speaking to him and saying, "These are the fields in which the Shepherds watched, and that rocky pathway leads up the slope to Bethlehem."

At the sound of the voice Isidore hastily looked round, and behind him was the pilgrim, and yet he knew that it was not truly the pilgrim, but an Angel disguised in pilgrim's weeds. And when he would have fallen at the Angel's feet, the Angel stopped him and said, "Be not afraid; I have been sent to show thee all the holy places that thy heart has longed to see."

On valley and hill and field and stream there now shone so clear and wonderful a light that even a long way off the very flowers by the roadside were distinctly visible. Without effort and without weariness Isidore glided from place to place as though it were a dream. And I cannot tell the half of what he saw, for the Angel took him to the village where Jesus was a little child, which is called Nazareth, "the flower-village;" and he showed him the River Jordan flowing through dark green woods, and Hermon the high mountain, glittering with snow (and the snow of that mountain is exceeding old), and the blue Lake of Gennesareth, with its fishing-craft, and the busy town of Capernaum on the great road to Damascus, and Nain where Jesus watched the little children playing at funerals and marriages in the market-place, and the wilderness where He was with the wild beasts, and Bethany where Lazarus lived and died and was brought to life again (and in the fields of Bethany Isidore gathered a bunch of wild flowers), and Jerusalem the holy city, and Gethsemane with its aged silver-grey olive-trees, and the hill of Calvary, where in the darkness a great cry went up to heaven: "Why hast Thou forsaken me?" and the new tomb in the white rock among the myrtles and rose-trees in the garden.

There was no place that Isidore had desired to see that was denied to him. And in all these places he saw the children's children of the children of those who had looked on the face of the Saviour—men and women and little ones—going to and fro in strangely coloured clothing, in the manner of those who had sat down on the green grass and been fed with bread and fishes. And at the thought of this Isidore wept.

"Why dost thou weep?" the Angel asked.

"I weep that I was not alive to look on the face of the Lord."

Then suddenly, as though it were a dream, they were on the sea-shore, and it was morning. And Isidore saw on the sparkling sea a fisher-ship drifting a little way from the shore, but there was no one in it; and on the shore a boat was aground; and half on the sand and half in the wash of the sea there were swathes of brown nets filled with a hundred great fish which flounced and glittered in the sun; and on the sand there was a coal fire with fish broiling on it, and on one side of the fire seven men—one of them kneeling and shivering in his drenched fisher's coat—and on the other side of the fire a benign and majestic figure, on whom the men were gazing in great joy and awe. And Isidore, knowing that this was the Lord, gazed too at Christ standing there in the sun.

And this was what he beheld: a man of lofty stature and most grave and beautiful countenance. His eyes were blue and very brilliant, his cheeks were slightly tinged with red, and his hair was of the ruddy golden colour of wine. From the top of his head to his ears it was straight and without radiance; but from his ears to his shoulders and down his back it fell in shining curls and clusters.

Again all was suddenly changed, and Isidore and the Angel were alone.

"Thou hast seen," said the Angel; "give me thy hand so that thou shalt not forget."

Isidore stretched out his hand, and the Angel opened it, and turning the palm upward, struck it. Isidore groaned with the sharp pain of the stroke, and sank into unconsciousness.

When he awoke in the morning the sun was high in the heavens, and the pilgrim had departed on his way. But the hut was filled with a heavenly fragrance, and on his bed Isidore perceived the wild flowers that he had plucked in the fields of Bethany—red anemones and blue lupins and yellow marigolds, with many others more sweet and lovely than the flowers that grew in the fields or Spain.

"Then surely," he cried, "it was not merely a dream."

And looking at his hand, he saw that the palm bore blue tracings such as one sees on the arms of wanderers and seafaring men. These marks, Isidore learned afterwards, were the Hebrew letters that spelt the name "JERUSALEM."

As long as he lived those letters recalled to his mind all the marvels that had been shown him. And they did more than this, for whenever his eyes fell on them he said, "Blessed be the promise of the Lord the Redeemer of Israel, who hath us in His care for evermore!"

Now these are the words of that promise:

"Can a woman forget her sucking child, that she should not have compassion on the son of her womb? Yea, they may forget, yet will I not forget thee. Behold, I have engraven thee upon the palms of my hands."

THE ANCIENT GODS PURSUING

I will now tell of Hilary and his companions, who came over the snowy passes of the Alps, and carried the lamp of faith into the north; and this was in the days of the ancient gods. Many of their shrines had Hilary overturned, and broken their images, and cut down their sacred trees, and denied their wells of healing. Wherefore terrible phantoms pursued him in his dreams, and in the darkness, and in the haunted ways of the woods and mountains. At one time it was the brute-god Pan, who sought to madden him with the terror of his piping in desolate places; at another it was the sun-god Apollo, who threatened him with fiery arrows in the parching heat of noon; or it was Pallas Athene, who appeared to him in visions, and shook in his face the Gorgon's head, which turns to stone all living creatures who look on it. But the holy Bishop made the sign of the cross of the Lord, and the right arm of their power was broken, and their malice could not harm him.

The holy men traversed the mountains by that Roman road which climbed up the icy rocks and among the snowy peaks of the Mountain of Jove, and at sundown they came to that high temple of Jove which had crowned the pass for many centuries. The statue of the great father-god of Rome had been hurled down the ravine into the snow-drift, and his altar had been flung into the little wintry mere which shivers in the pass, and his last priest had died of old age a lifetime ago; and the temple was now but a cold harbour for merchants and soldiers and wandering men.

Here in the freezing air the apostles rested from their journey, but in the dead of the night Hilary was awakened by a clamour of forlorn voices, and opening his eyes he saw the mighty father-god of Olympus looking down upon him with angry brows, and brandishing in his hand red flashes of lightning. In no way daunted, the Bishop sprang to his feet, and cried in a loud voice, "In the name of Him who was crucified, depart to your torments!" And at the sound of that cry the colossal figure of the god wavered and broke like a mountain cloud when it crumbles in the wind, and glimmering shapes of goddesses and nymphs flitted past, sighing and lamenting; and the Bishop saw no longer anything but the sharp cold stars, and the white peaks and the ridges of the mountains.

When they had descended and reached the green valleys, they came at length to a great lake, blue and beautiful to look upon, and here they sojourned for a while. It was a fair and pleasant land, but the people were rude and barbarous, and drove them away with stones when they would enter their hamlets. So, as they needed food, Hilary bade his companions gather berries and wild herbs, and he himself set snares for birds, and wove a net to cast into the lake, and made himself a raft of pine-trees, from which he might cast it the more easily.

One night as he floated on this raft in the starlight, he heard the voice of the Spirit of the Peak calling to the Spirit of the Mere. And the Spirit of the Mere answered, "Speak, I am listening." Then the Mountain Spirit cried, "Arise, then, and come to my aid; alone I cannot chase away these men who are driving out all the ancient gods from their shrines in the land." The Water Spirit answered, "Of what avail is our strength against theirs? Here on the starry waters is one whose nets I cannot break, and whose boat I cannot overturn. Without ceasing he prays, and never are his eyes closed in slumber." Then Hilary arose on his raft, and raising his hand to heaven cried against the Spirit of the Peak and the Spirit of the Mere: "In the name of Him crucified, be silent for evermore, and leave these hills and waters to the servants of God." And these creatures of evil were stricken dumb, and they fled in dismay, making a great moaning and sobbing, and the dolorous sound was as that of the wind in the pines and the water on the rocks.

Then Hilary and his companions fared away into the north, through the Grey Waste, which is a wild and deserted country where in the olden time vast armies had passed with fire and sword; and now the field had turned into wildwood and morass, and the rich townsteads were barrows of ruins and ashes overgrown with brambles, and had been given for a lodging to the savage beasts. The name of this waste was more terrible than the place, for the season was sweet and gracious, and of birds and fish and herbs and wild honey there was no dearth. They were now no longer harassed by the phantoms of the ancient gods, or by the evil spirits of the unblessed earth. Thus for many long leagues was their journey made easy for them.

Now it chanced, when they had reached the further edge of this region, that as they went one night belated along a green riding, which in the old time had been a spacious paved causeway between rich cities, they heard the music of a harp, more marvellously sweet and solacing than any mortal minstrel may make; and sweet dream-voices sighed to them "Follow, follow!" and they felt their feet drawn as by enchantment; and as they yielded to the magical power, a soft shining filled the dusky air, and they saw that the ground was covered with soft deep grass and brilliant flowers, and the trees were of the colour of gold and silver. So in strange gladness, and feeling neither hunger nor fatigue, they went forward through the hours of the night till the dawn, wondering what angelic ministry was thus beguiling them of hardship and pain. But with the first gleam of the dawn the music ceased amid mocking laughter, the vision of lovely woodland vanished away, and in the grey light they found themselves on the quaking green edges of a deep and dangerous marsh. Hilary, when he saw this, groaned in spirit and said: "O dear sons, we have deserved this befooling and misguidance, for have we not forgotten the behest of our Master, 'Watch and pray lest ye enter into temptation'?"

Now when after much toilsomeness they had won clear of that foul tract of morass and quagmire, they came upon vast herds of swine grubbing beneath the oaks, and with them savage-looking swineherds scantily clad in skins. Still further north they caught sight of the squalid hovels and wood piles of charcoal burners; and still they pursued their way till they cleared the dense forest and beheld before them a long range of hills blue in the distant air. Towards sundown they came on a stony moorland, rough with heather and bracken and tufts of bent; and when there was but one long band of red light parting the distant land from the low sky, they descried a range of thick posts standing high and black against the red in the heavens. As they drew near, these, they discovered, were the huge granite pillars of a great ring of stone and of an avenue which led up to it; and in the midst of the ring was a mighty flat stone borne up on three stout pillars, so that it looked like a wondrous stone house of some strong folk of the beginning of days.

"This, too, companions," said Hilary, "is a temple of false gods. Very ancient gods of a world gone by are these, and it may be they have been long dead like their worshippers, and their names are no more spoken in the world. Further we may not go this night; but on these stones we shall put the sign of the blessed tree of our redemption, and in its shelter shall we sleep."

As they slept that night in the lee of the stones Hilary saw in a dream the place wherein they lay; and the great stones, he was aware, were not true stones of the rock, but petrified trees, and in his spirit he knew that these trees of stone were growths of that Forbidden Tree with the fruit of which the Serpent tempted our first mother in Paradise. On the morrow when they rose, he strove to overthrow the huge pillars, but to this labour their strength was not equal.

This same day was the day of St. John, the longest in all the year, and they travelled far, till at last in the long afternoon they arrived in sight of a cluster of little homesteads, clay huts thatched with bracken and fenced about with bushes of poison-thorn, and of tilled crofts sloping down the hillside to a clear river wending through the valley.

As Hilary and his companions approached they saw that it was a day of rejoicing and merry-making among the people, for they were all abroad, feasting and drinking from great mead horns in the open air, and shouting barbarous songs to the noise of rude instruments. When it grew to such duskiness as there may be in a midsummer night countless fires were lit, near at hand and far away, on the hills around; and on the ridges above the river children ran about with blazing brands of pine-wood, and young men and maidens gathered at the flaming beacon. Wheels, too, wrapped round tire and spoke with straw and flax smeared with pine-tree gum, were set alight and sent rolling down the hill to the river, amid wild cries and clapping of hands. Some of the wheels went awry and were stayed among the boulders; on some the flames died out; but there were those which reached the river and plunged into the water and were extinguished; and the owners of these last deemed themselves fortunate in their omens, for these fiery wheels were images of the sun in heaven, and their course to the river was the forecasting of his prosperous journey through the year to come.

Thus these outland people held their festival, and Hilary marvelled to see the many fires, for he had not known that the land held so many folk. But now when it was time for the wayfarers to cast about in their minds how and where they should pass the night, there came to them a stranger, a grave and seemly man clad in the manner of the Romans, and he bowed low to them, and said: "O saintly men, the Lady Pelagia hath heard of your coming into this land, and she knows that you have come to teach men the new faith, for she is a great lady, mistress of vast demesnes, and many messengers bring her tidings of all that happens. She bids me greet you humbly and prevail on you to come and abide this night in her house, which is but a little way from here."

"Is your lady of Rome?" asked Hilary.

"From Rome she came hither," said the messenger, "but aforetime she was of Greece, and she hath great friendship for all wise and holy men."

The wayfarers were surprised to hear of this lady, but they were rejoiced that, after such long wandering, there was some one to welcome them where least they had expected word of welcome, and they followed the messenger.

Horn lantern in hand he led them through the warm June darkness, and on the way answered many questions as to the folk of these parts, and their strange worship of sun and moon and wandering light of heaven; "but in a brief while,"

William Canton

he said, "all these heathen matters will be put by, when you have taught them the new faith."

Up a gloomily wooded rise he guided them, till they passed into the radiance of a house lit with many lamps and cressets, and the house, they saw, was of fair marble such as are the houses of the patricians of Rome; and many beautiful slaves, lightly clad and garlanded with roses, brought them water in silver bowls and white linen wherewith they might cleanse themselves from the dust of their travel.

In a little the Lady Pelagia received them and bade them welcome, and prayed them to make her poor house their dwelling-place while they sojourned in that waste of heathendom. Then she led them to a repast which had been made ready for them.

Of all the gracious and lovely women in the round of the kingdoms of the earth none is, or hath been, or will be, more marvellous in beauty or in sweetness of approach than this lady; and she made Hilary sit beside her, and questioned him of the Saints in the Queen City of the world, and of his labours and his long wanderings, and the perils through which he and his companions had come. All the while she spoke her starry eyes shed soft light on his face, and she leaned towards him her lovely head and fragrant bosom, drinking in his words with a look of longing. The companions whispered among themselves that assuredly this was rather an Angel of Paradise than a mortal creature of the dust of the earth, which to-day is as a flower in its desirableness and to-morrow is blown about all the ways of men's feet. Even the good Bishop felt his heart moved towards her with a strange tenderness, so sweet was the thought of her youth and her beauty and her goodness and humility.

Sitting in this fashion at table and conversing, and the talk now veering to this and now to that, the Lady Pelagia said: "This longest of the days has been to me the most happy, holy fathers, for it has brought you to the roof of a sinful woman, and you have not disdained the service she has offered you in all lowliness of heart. A long and, it may be, a dangerous labour lies before you, for the folk of this land are fierce and quick to violence; but here you may ever refresh yourselves from toil and take your rest, free from danger. No loving offices or lowly observance, no, nor ought you desire is there that you may not have for the asking—or without the asking, if it be given me to know your wish unspoken."

Hilary and the brethren bowed low at these gracious words, and thought within themselves: Of a truth this may be a woman, but she is no less an Angel for our strength and solacement.

"In the days to come," said the lady, "there will be many things to ask and learn from you, but now ere this summer night draws to end let me have knowledge of divine things from thee, most holy father, for thou art wise and canst answer all my questionings."

And Hilary smiled gravely, not ill pleased at her words of praise, and said: "Ask, daughter."

"First tell me," she said, "which of all the small things God has made in the world is the most excellent?"

Hilary wondered and mused, but could find no answer; and when he would have said so, the voice which came from his lips spoke other words than those he intended to speak, so that instead of saying "This is a question I cannot answer," his voice said: "Of all small things made by God, most excellent is the face of man and woman; for among all the faces of the children of Adam not any one hath ever been wholly like any other; and there in smallest space God has placed all the senses of the body; and it is in the face that we see, as in a glass, darkly, all that can be seen of the invisible soul within."

The companions listened marvelling, but Hilary marvelled no less than they.

"It is well answered," said the lady, "and yet it seemed to me there was one thing more excellent. But let me ask again: What earth is nearest to heaven?"

Again Hilary mused and was silent. Then, once more, the voice which was his voice and yet spoke words which he did not think to speak, gave the answer: "The body of Him who died on the tree to save us, for He was of our flesh, and our flesh is earth of the earth."

"That too is well answered," said the lady, who had grown pale and gazed on the Bishop with great gloomy eyes; "and yet I had thought of another answer. Once more let me question you: What is the distance between heaven and earth?"

Then for the third time was Hilary unable to reply, but the voice answered for him, in stern and menaceful tones: "Who can tell us that more certainly than Lucifer who fell from heaven?"

With a bitter cry the Lady Pelagia rose from her seat, and raised her beautiful white arms above her head; but the voice continued: "Breathe on her, Hilary—breathe the breath of the name of Christ!"

And the Bishop, rising, breathed on the white lovely face the breath of the holy name; and in an instant the starry eyes were darkened, and the spirit and flower of life perished in her sweet body; and the companions saw no longer the Lady Pelagia, but in her stead a statue of white marble. At a glance Hilary knew it for a statue of the goddess whom men in Rome called Venus and in Greece Aphrodite, and with a shudder he remembered that another of her names was Pelagia, the Lady of the Sea. But, swifter even than that thought, it seemed to them as though the statue were smitten by an invisible hand, for it reeled and fell, shattered to fragments; and the lights were extinguished, and the air of the summer night blew upon their faces, and in the east, whence cometh our hope, there was a glimmer of dawn.

Praying fervently, and bewailing the brief joy they had taken in the beauty of that dreadful goddess, they waited for light to guide them from that evil place.

When the day broadened they perceived that they were in the midst of the ruins of an ancient Roman city, overgrown with bush and tree. Around them lay, amid beds of nettles and great dock leaves, and darnel and tangles of briars, and tall foxgloves and deadly nightshade, the broken pillars of a marble temple. This had been the fair house, lit with lamps, wherein they had sat at feast. Close beside them were scattered the white fragments of the image of the beautiful Temptress.

As they turned to depart three grey wolves snarled at them from the ruins, but an unseen hand held these in leash, and Hilary and his companions went on their way unharmed.

William Canton

THE DREAM OF THE WHITE LARK

This was a thing that happened long and long ago, in the glimmering morning of the Christian time in Erinn. And it may have happened to the holy Maedog of Ferns, or to Enan the Angelic, or it may have been Molasius of Devenish—I cannot say. But over the windy sea in his small curragh of bull's hide the Saint sailed far away to the southern land; and for many a month he travelled afoot through the dark forests, and the sunny corn-lands, and over the snowy mountain horns, and along the low shores between the olive-grey hills and the blue sea, till at last he came in sight of a great and beautiful city glittering on the slopes and ridges of seven hills.

"What golden city may this be?" he asked of the dark-eyed market folk whom he met on the long straight road which led across the open country.

"It is the city of Rome," they answered him, wondering at his ignorance. But the Saint, when he heard those words, fell on his knees and kissed the ground.

"Hail to thee, most holy city!" he cried; "hail, thou queen of the world, red with the roses of the martyrs and white with the lilies of the virgins; hail, blessed goal of my long wandering!"

And as he entered the city his eyes were bright with joy, and his heart seemed to lift his weary feet on wings of gladness.

There he sojourned through the autumn and the winter, visiting all the great churches and the burial-places of the early Christians in the Catacombs, and communing with the good and wise men in many houses of religion. Once he conversed with the great Pope whose name was Gregory, and told him of his brethren in the beloved isle in the western waters.

When once more the leaf of the fig-tree opened its five fingers, and the silvery bud of the vine began to unfurl, the Saint prepared to return home. And once more he went to the mighty Pope, to take his leave and to ask a blessing for himself and his brethren, and to beg that he might bear away with him to the brotherhood some precious relic of those who had shed their blood for the Cross.

As he made that request in the green shadowy garden on the Hill Caelian, the Pope smiled, and, taking a clod of common earth from the soil, gave it to the Saint, saying, "Then take this with thee," and when the Saint expressed his surprise at so strange a relic, the Servant of the Servants of God took back the earth and crushed it in his hand, and with amazement the Saint saw that blood began to trickle from it between the fingers of the Pope.

Marvelling greatly, the Saint kissed the holy pontiff's hand, and bade him farewell; and going to and fro among those he knew, he collected money, and, hiring a ship, he filled it with the earth of Rome, and sailed westward through the Midland Sea, and bent his course towards the steadfast star in the north, and so at last reached the beloved green island of his home.

William Canton

In the little graveyard about the fair church of his brotherhood he spread the earth which had drunk the blood of the martyrs, so that the bodies of those who died in the Lord might await His coming in a blessed peace.

Now it happened that but a few days after his return the friend of his boyhood, a holy brother who had long shared with him the companionship of the cloister, migrated from this light, and when the last requiem had been sung and the sacred earth had covered in the dead, the Saint wept bitterly for the sake of the lost love and the unforgotten years.

And at night he fell asleep, still weeping for sorrow. And in his sleep he saw, as in a dream, the grey stone church with its round tower and the graveyard sheltered by the woody hills; but behold! in the graveyard tall trees sprang in lofty spires from the earth of Rome, and reached into the highest heavens; and these trees were like trees of green and golden and ruddy fire, for they were red with the blossoms of life, and every green leaf quivered with bliss, like a green flame; and among the trees, on a grassy sod at their feet, sat a white lark, singing clear and loud, and he knew that the lark was the soul of the friend of his boyhood.

As he listened to its song, he understood its unearthly music; and these were the words of its singing: "Do not weep any more for me; it is pity for thy sorrow which keeps me here on the grass. If thou wert not so unhappy I should fly."

And when the Saint awoke his grief had fallen from him, and he wept no more for the dead man whom he loved.

THE HERMIT OF THE PILLAR

On one of the hills near the city of Ancyra Basil the hermit stood day and night on a pillar of stone forty feet high, praying and weeping for his own sins and for the sins of the world.

A gaunt, dark figure, far up in the blue Asian sky, he stood there for a sign and a warning to all men that our earthly life is short, whether for wickedness or repentance; that the gladness and the splendour of the world are but a fleeting pageant; that in but a little while the nations should tremble before the coming of the Lord in His power and majesty. Little heed did the rich and dissolute people of that city give to his cry of doom; and of the vast crowds who came about the foot of his pillar, the greater number thought but to gaze on the wonder of a day, though some few did pitch their tents hard by, and spent the time of their sojourn in prayer and the lamentation of hearts humbled and contrite.

Now, in the third year of his testimony, as Basil was rapt in devotion, with hands and face uplifted to the great silent stars, an Angel, clothed in silver and the blue-green of the night, stood in front of him in the air, and said: "Descend from thy pillar, and get thee away far westward; and there thou shalt learn what is for thy good."

William Canton

Without delay or doubt Basil descended, and stole away alone in the hush before the new day, and took the winding ways of the hills, and thereafter went down into the low country of the plain to seaward.

After long journeying among places and people unknown, he crossed the running seas which part the eastern world from the world of the west, and reached the City of the Golden Horn, Byzantium; and there for four months he lived on a pillar overlooking the city and the narrow seas, and cried his cry of doom and torment. At the end of the fourth month the Angel once more came to him and bade him descend and go further.

So with patience and constancy of soul he departed between night and light, and pursued his way for many months till he had got to the ancient city of Treves. There, among the ruins of a temple of the heathen goddess Diana, he found a vast pillar of marble still erect, and the top of this he thought to make his home and holy watch-tower. Wherefore he sought out the Bishop of the city and asked his leave and blessing, and the Bishop, marvelling greatly at his zeal and austerity, gave his consent.

The people of Treves were amazed at what they considered his madness; but they gave him no hindrance, nor did they molest him in any way. Indeed, in no long time the fame of his penance was noised abroad, and multitudes came, as they had come at Ancyra, to see with their own eyes what there was of truth in the strange story they had heard. Afterwards, too, many came out of sorrow for sin and an ardent desire of holiness; and others brought their sick and maimed and afflicted, in the hope that the Hermit might be able to cure their ailments, or give them assuagement of their sufferings. Many of these, in truth, Basil sent away cleansed and made whole by the virtue of his touch or of the blessing he bestowed upon them.

Now, though there were many pillar-hermits in the far eastern land, this was the first that had ever been seen in the west, and after him there were but few others.

A strange and well-nigh incredible thing it seemed, to look upon this man on the height of his pillar, preaching and praying constantly, and enduring night and day the inclemency of the seasons and the weariness and discomfort of his narrow standing place. For the pillar, massive as it was, was so narrow where the marble curved over in big acanthus leaves at the four corners that he had not room to lie down at length to sleep; and indeed he slept but little, considering slumber a waste of the time of prayer, and the dreams of sleep so many temptations to beguile the soul into false and fugitive pleasures. No shelter was there from the wind, but he was bare as a stone in the field to the driving rain and the blaze of the sun at noon; and in winter the frost was bitter to flesh and blood, and the snow fell like flakes or white fire. His only clothing was a coat of sheepskin; about his neck hung a heavy chain of iron, in token that he was a thrall and bondsman of the Lord Christ, and each Friday he wore an iron crown of thorns, in painful memory of Christ's passion and His sorrowful death upon the tree. Once a day he ate a little rye bread, and once he drank a little water.

No man could say whether he was young or aged; and the mother who had borne him a little babe at her bosom, and had watched him grow to boyhood, could not have recognised him, for he had been burnt black by the sun and the frost, and the weather had bleached his hair and beard till they looked like lichens on an ancient forest-tree, and the crown of thorns had scarred his brow, and the links of the chain had galled his neck and shoulders.

For three summers and three winters he endured this stricken life with cheerful fortitude, counting his sufferings as great gain if through them he might secure the crown of celestial glory which God has woven for His elect. Remembering all his prayers and supplications, and the long martyrdom of his body, it was hard for him, at times, to resist the assurance that he must have won a golden seat among the blessed.

"For who, O Lord Christ!" he cried, with trembling hands outstretched, and dim eyes weeping, "who hath taken up Thy cross as I have done, and the anguish of the thorns and the nails, and the parched sorrow of Thy thirst, and the wounding of Thy blessed body, and borne them for years twenty and three, and shown them as I have shown them to the sun and stars and the four winds, high up between heaven and earth, that men might be drawn to Thee, and carried them across the world from the outmost East to the outmost West? Surely, Lord God! Thou hast written my name in Thy Book of Life, and hast set for me a happy place in the heavens. Surely, all I have and am I have given Thee; and all that a worm of the earth may do have I done! If in anything I have failed, show me, Lord, I beseech Thee, wherein I have come short. If any man there be more worthy in Thine eyes, let me, too, set eyes upon him, that I may learn of him how I may the better please Thee. Teach me, Lord, that which I know not, for Thou alone knowest and art wise!"

As Basil was praying thus in the hour before dawn, once more the Angel, clothed in silver and blue-green, as though it had been a semblance of the starry night, came to him, and said: "Give me thy hand;" and Basil touched the hand celestial, and the Angel drew him from his pillar, and placed him on the ground, and said: "This is that land of the west in which thou art to learn what is for thy good. Take for staff this piece of tree, and follow this road till thou reachest the third milestone; and there, in the early light, thou shalt meet him who can instruct thee. For a sign, thou shalt know the man by the little maid of seven years who helpeth him to drive the geese. But the man, though young, may teach one who is older than he, and he is one who is greatly pleasing in God's eyes."

The clear light was glittering on the dewy grass and the wet bushes when Basil reached the third milestone. He heard the distant sound as of a shepherd piping, and he saw that the road in front of him was crowded for near upon a quarter of a mile with a great gathering of geese—fully two thousand they numbered—feeding in the grass and rushes, and cackling, and hustling each other aside, and clacking their big orange-coloured bills, as they waddled slowly onward towards the city.

Among them walked a nut-brown little maiden of seven, clad in a green woollen tunic, with bright flaxen hair and innocent blue eyes, and bare brown legs, and feet shod in shoes of hide. In her hand she carried a long hazel wand, with which she kept in rule the large grey and white geese.

As the flock came up to the Hermit, she gazed at him with her sweet wondering eyes, for never had she seen so strange and awful a man as this, with his sheepskin dress and iron chain and crown of thorns, and skin burnt black, and bleached hair and dark brows stained with blood. For a moment she stood still in awe and fear, but the Hermit raised his hand, and blessed her, and smiled upon her; and even in that worn and disfigured face the light in the Hermit's eyes as he smiled was tender and beautiful; and the child ceased to fear, and passed slowly along, still gazing at him and smiling in return.

In the rear of the great multitude of geese came a churl, tall and young, and comely enough for all his embrowning in the

William Canton

sun and wind, and his unkempt hair and rude dress. It was he who made the music, playing on pan's-pipes to lighten the way, and quickening with his staff the loiterers of his flock.

When he perceived the Hermit he stayed his playing, for he bethought him, Is not this the saintly man of whose strange penance and miracles of healing the folk talk in rustic huts and hamlets far scattered? But when they drew nigh to each other, the Hermit bowed low to the Gooseherd, and addressed him: "Give me leave to speak a little with thee, good brother; for an Angel of heaven hath told me of thee, and fain would I converse with thee. Twenty years and three have I served the King of Glory in supplication and fasting and tribulation of spirit, and yet I lack that which thou canst teach me. Now tell me, I beseech thee, what works, what austerities, what prayers have made thee so acceptable to God."

A dark flush rose on the Goose-herd's cheeks as he listened, but when he answered it was in a grave and quiet voice: "It ill becomes an aged man to mock and jeer at the young, nor is it more seemly that the holy should gibe at the poor."

"Dear son in Christ," said the Hermit, "I do not gibe or mock at thee. By the truth of the blessed tree, I was told of thee by an Angel in the very night which is now over and gone, and was bidden to question thee. Wherefore be not wrathful, but answer me truly, I beg of thy charity."

The Goose-herd shook his head. "This is a matter beyond me," he replied. "All my work, since thou askest of my work, hath been the tending and rearing of geese and driving them to market. From the good marsh lands at the foot of the hills out west I drive them, and the distance is not small, for, sleeping and resting by boulder and tree, for five days are we on the way. Slow of foot goeth your goose when he goeth not by water, and it profits neither master nor herd to stint them of their green food. And all my prayer hath been that I might get them safe to market, none missing or fallen dead by the way, and that I might sell them speedily and at good price, and so back to the fens again. What more is there to say?"

"In thy humility thou hidest something from me," said the Hermit, and he fixed his eyes thoughtfully on the young man's face.

"Nay, I have told thee all that is worth the telling."

"Then hast thou always lived this life?" the Hermit asked.

"Ever since I was a small lad—such a one as the little maid in front, and she will be in her seventh year, or it may be a little older. Before me was my father goose-herd; and he taught me the windings of the journey to the city, and the best resting-places, and the ways of geese, and the meaning of their cries, and what pleaseth them and serveth flesh and feather, and how they should be driven. And now, in turn, I teach the child, for there be goose-girls as well as men."

"Is she then thy young sister, or may it be that she is thy daughter?"

"Neither young sister nor daughter is she," replied the Herd, "and yet in truth she is both sister and daughter."

"Wilt thou tell me how that may be?" asked the Hermit.

"It is shortly told," said the Herd. "Robbers broke into their poor and lonely house by the roadside and slew father and mother and left them dead, but the babe at the breast they had not slain, and this was she."

"Didst thou find her?" asked the Hermit.

"Ay, on a happy day I found her; a feeble little thing bleating like a lambkin forlorn beside its dead dam."

"And thy wife, belike, or thy mother, reared her?"

"Nay," said the Herd, "for my mother was dead, and no wife have I. I reared her myself—my little white gooseling; and she throve and waxed strong of heart and limb, and merry and brown of favour, as thou hast seen."

"Thou must have been thyself scantly a man in those days," said the Hermit.

"Younger than to-day," replied the Herd; "but I was ever big of limb and plentiful of my inches."

"And hath she not been often since a burthen to thee, and a weariness in the years?"

"She hath been a care in the cold winter, and a sorrow in her sickness with her teeth—for no man, I wot, can help a small child when the teeth come through the gum, and she can but cry ah! ah! and hath no words to tell what she aileth."

"Why didst thou do all this?" asked the Hermit. "What hath been thy reward? Or for what reward dost thou look?"

The Goose-herd looked at him blankly for a moment; then his face brightened. "Surely," he said, "to see her as she goes on her way, a bright, brown little living thing, with her clear hair and glad eyes, is a goodly reward. And a goodly reward is it to think of her growth, and to mind me of the days when she could not walk and I bore her whithersoever I went; and of the days when she could but take faltering steps and was soon fain to climb into my arms and sit upon my neck; and of the days when we first fared together with the geese to market and I cut her her first hazel stick; and in truth of all the days that she hath been with me since I found her."

As the Goose-herd spoke the tears rose in the Hermit's eyes and rolled slowly down his cheeks; and when the young man ceased, he said: "O son, now I know why thou art so pleasing in the eyes of God. Early hast thou learned the love which gives all and asks nothing, which suffereth long and is ever kind, and this I have not learned. A small thing and too common it seemed to me, but now I see that it is holier than austerities, and availeth more than fasting, and is the prayer of prayers. Late have I sought thee, thou ancient truth, late have I found thee, thou ancient beauty; yet even in the gloaming of my days may there still be light enough to win my way home. Farewell, good brother; and be God tender and pitiful to thee as thou hast been tender and pitiful to the little child."

"Farewell, holy man!" replied the Herd, regarding him with a perplexed look, for the life and austerities of the Hermit were a mystery he could not understand.

Then going on his way, he laid the pan's-pipes to his lips and whistled a pleasant music as he strode after his geese.

William Canton

KENACH'S LITTLE WOMAN

As the holy season of Lent drew nigh, the Abbot Kenach felt a longing such as a bird of passage feels in the south when the first little silvery buds on the willow begin here to break their ruddy sheaths, and the bird thinks to-morrow it will be time to fly over-seas to the land where it builds its nest in pleasant croft or under the shelter of homely eaves. And Kenach said, "Levabo oculos—I will lift up mine eyes unto the hills from whence cometh my help;" for every year it was his custom to leave his abbey and fare through the woods to the hermitage on the mountain-side, so that he might spend the forty days of fasting and prayer in the heart of solitude.

Now on the day which is called the Wednesday or Ashes he set out, but first he heard the mass of remembrance and led his monks to the altar steps, and knelt there in great humility to let the priest sign his forehead with a cross of ashes. And on the forehead of each of the monks the ashes were smeared in the form of a cross, and each time the priest made the sign he repeated the words, "Remember, man, that thou art dust, and unto dust thou shalt return."

So with the ashes still on his brow and with the remembrance of the end of earthly days in his soul, he bent his steps towards the hermitage; and as he was now an aged man and nowise strong, Diarmait, one of the younger brethren, accompanied him in case any mischance should befall.

They passed through the cold forest, where green there was none, unless it were the patches of moss and the lichens on the rugged tree-trunks and tufts of last year's grass, but here and there the white blossoms of the snowdrops peered out. The dead grey leaves and dry twigs crackled and snapped under their feet with such a noise as a wood fire makes when it is newly lighted; and that was all the warmth they had on their wayfaring.

The short February day was closing in as they climbed among the boulders and withered bracken on the mountain-side, and at last reached the entrance of a cavern hollowed in the rock and fringed with ivy. This was the hermitage. The Abbot hung his bell on a thick ivy-bough in the mouth of the cave; and they knelt and recited vespers and compline; and thrice the Abbot struck the bell to scare away the evil spirits of the night; and they entered and lay down to rest.

Hard was the way of their sleeping; for they lay not on wool or on down, neither on heather or bracken, nor yet on dry leaves, but their sides came against the cold stone, and under the head of each there was a stone for pillow. But being weary with the long journey they slept sound, and felt nothing of the icy mouth of the wind blowing down the mountain-side.

Within an hour of daybreak, when the moon was setting, they were awakened by the wonderful singing of a bird, and they rose for matins and strove not to listen, but so strangely sweet was the sound in the keen moonlight morning that they could not forbear. The moon set, and still in the dark sang the bird, and the grey light came, and the bird ceased; and when it was white day they saw that all the ground and every stalk of bracken was hoary with frost, and every ivy-leaf was

William Canton

crusted white round the edge, but within the edge it was all glossy green.

"What bird is this that sings so sweet before day in the bitter cold?" said the Abbot. "Surely no bird at all, but an Angel from heaven waking us from the death of sleep."

"It is the blackbird, Domine Abbas," said the young monk; "often they sing thus in February, however cold it may be."

"O soul, O Diarmait, is it not wonderful that the senseless small creatures should praise God so sweetly in the dark, and in the light before the dark, while we are fain to lie warm and forget His praise?" And afterwards he said, "Gladly could I have listened to that singing, even till to-morrow was a day; and yet it was but the singing of a little earth wrapped in a handful of feathers. O soul, tell me what it must be to listen to the singing of an Angel, a portion of heaven wrapped in the glory of God's love!"

Of the forty days thirty went by, and oftentimes now, when no wind blew, it was bright and delightsome among the rocks, for the sun was gaining strength, and the days were growing longer, and the brown trees were being speckled with numberless tiny buds of white and pale green, and wild flowers were springing between the boulders and through the mountain turf.

Hard by the cave there was a low wall of rock covered with ivy, and as Diarmait chanced to walk near it, a brown bird darted out from among the leaves. The young monk looked at the place from which it had flown, and behold! among the leaves and the hairy sinews of the ivy there was a nest lined with grass, and in the nest there were three eggs—pale-green with reddish spots. And Diarmait knew the bird and knew the eggs, and he told the Abbot, who came noiselessly, and looked with a great love at the open house and the three eggs of the mother blackbird.

"Let us not walk too near, my son," he said, "lest we scare the mother from her brood, and so silence beforehand some of the music of the cold hours before the day." And he lifted his hand and blessed the nest and the bird, saying, "And He shall bless thy bread and thy water." After that it was very seldom they went near the ivy.

Now after days of clear and benign weather a shrill wind broke out from beneath the North Star, and brought with it snow and sleet and piercing cold. And the woods howled for distress of the storm, and the grey stones of the mountain chattered with discomfort. Harsh cold and sleeplessness were their lot in the cave, and as he shivered, the Abbot bethought him of the blackbird in her nest, and of the wet flakes driving in between the leaves of the ivy and stinging her brown wings and patient bosom. And lifting his head from his pillow of stone he prayed the Lord of the elements to have the bird in His gentle care, saying, "How excellent is Thy loving-kindness, O God! therefore the children of men put their trust under the shadow of Thy wings."

Then after a little while he said, "Look out into the night, O son, and tell me if yet the storm be abated."

And Diarmait, shuddering, went to the mouth of the cavern, and stood there gazing and calling in a low voice, "Domine Abbas! My Lord Abbot! My Lord Abbot!"

Kenach rose quickly and went to him, and as they looked out the sleet beat on their faces, but in the midst of the storm there was a space of light, as though it were moonshine, and the light streamed from an Angel, who stood near the wall of rock with outspread wings, and sheltered the blackbird's nest from the wintry blast.

And the monks gazed at the shining loveliness of the Angel, till the wind fell and the snow ceased and the light faded away and the sharp stars came out and the night was still.

Now at sundown of the day that followed, when the Abbot was in the cave, the young monk, standing among the rocks, saw approaching a woman who carried a child in her arms; and crossing himself he cried aloud to her, "Come not any nearer; turn thy face to the forest, and go down."

"Nay," replied the woman, "for we seek shelter for the night, and food and the solace of fire for the little one."

"Go down, go down," cried Diarmait; "no woman may come to this hermitage."

"How canst thou say that, O monk?" said the woman. "Was the Lord Christ any worse than thou? Christ came to redeem woman no less than to redeem man. Not less did He suffer for the sake of woman than for the sake of man. Women gave service and tendance to Him and His Apostles. A woman it was who bore Him, else had men been left forlorn. It was a man who betrayed Him with a kiss; a woman it was who washed His feet with tears. It was a man who smote Him with a reed, but a woman who broke the alabaster box of precious ointment. It was a man who thrice denied Him; a woman stood by His cross. It was a woman to whom He first spoke on Easter morn, but a man thrust his hand into His side and put his finger in the prints of the nails before he would believe. And not less than men do women enter the heavenly kingdom. Why then shouldst thou drive my little child and me from thy hermitage?"

Then Kenach, who had heard all that was said, came forth

from the cave, and blessed the woman. "Well hast thou spoken, O daughter; come, and bring the small child with thee." And, turning to the young monk, he said, "O soul, O son, O Diarmait, did not God send His Angel out of high heaven to shelter the mother bird? And was not that, too, a little woman in feathers? But now hasten, and gather wood and leaves, and strike fire from the flint, and make a hearth before the cave, that the woman may rest and the boy have the comfort of the bright flame."

This was soon done, and by the fire sat the woman eating a little barley bread; but the child, who had no will to eat came round to the old man, and held out two soft hands to him. And the Abbot caught him up from the ground to his breast, and kissed his golden head, saying, "God bless thee sweet little son, and give thee a good life and a happy, and strength of thy small body, and, if it be His holy will, length of glad days; and ever mayest thou be a gladness and deep joy to thy mother."

Then, seeing that the woman was strangely clad in an outland garb of red and blue, and that she was tall, with a golden-hued skin and olive eyes, arched eyebrows very black, aquiline nose, and a rosy mouth, he said, "Surely, O daughter, thou art not of this land of Erinn in the sea, but art come out of the great world beyond?"

"Indeed, then, we have travelled far," replied the woman; "as thou sayest, out of the great world beyond. And now the twilight deepens upon us."

"Thou shalt sleep safe in the cave, O daughter, but we will rest here by the embers. My cloak of goats' hair shalt thou have, and such dry bracken and soft bushes as may be found."

William Canton

"There is no need," said the woman, "mere shelter is enough;" and she added in a low voice, "Often has my little son had no bed wherein he might lie."

Then she stretched out her arms to the boy, and once more the little one kissed the Abbot, and as he passed by Diarmait he put the palms of his hands against the face of the young monk, and said laughingly, "I do not think thou hadst any ill-will to us, though thou wert rough and didst threaten to drive us away into the woods."

And the woman lifted the boy on her arm, and rose and went towards the cavern; and when she was in the shadow of the rocks she turned towards the monks beside the fire, and said, "My son bids me thank you."

They looked up, and what was their astonishment to see a heavenly glory shining about the woman and her child in the gloom of the cave. And in his left hand the child carried a little golden image of the world, and round his head was a starry radiance, and his right hand was raised in blessing.

For such a while as it takes the shadow of a cloud to run across a rippling field of corn, for so long the vision remained; and then it melted into the darkness, even as a rainbow melts away into the rain.

On his face fell the Abbot, weeping for joy beyond words; but Diarmait was seized with fear and trembling till he remembered the way in which the child had pressed warm palms against his face and forgiven him.

The story of these things was whispered abroad, and ever since, in that part of Erinn in the sea, the mother blackbird is called Kenach's Little Woman.

And as for the stone on which the fire was lighted in front of the cave, rain rises quickly from it in mist and leaves it dry, and snow may not lie upon it, and even in the dead of winter it is warm to touch. And to this day it is called the Stone of Holy Companionship.

William Canton

GOLDEN APPLES AND ROSES RED

In the cruel days of old, when Diocletian was the Master of the World, and the believers in the Cross were maimed, and tortured with fire, and torn with iron hooks, and cast to the lions, and beheaded with the sword, Dorothea, a beautiful maiden of Caesarea, was brought before Sapricius, the Governor of Cappadocia, and commanded to forsake the Lord Christ and offer incense to the images of the false gods.

Though she was so young and so fair and tender, she stood unmoved by threats and entreaties, and when, with little pity on her youth and loveliness, Sapricius menaced her with the torment of the iron bed over a slow fire, she replied: "Do with me as you will. No pain shall I fear, so firm is my trust in Him for whom I am ready to die."

"Who, then, is this that has won thy love?" asked the Governor.

"It is Christ Jesus, the Son of God. Slay me, and I shall but the sooner be with Him in His Paradise, where there is no more pain, neither sorrow, but the tears are wiped from all eyes, and the roses are in bloom alway, and for ever the fruit of joy is on the trees."

"Thy words are but the babbling of madness," said the

Governor angrily.

"I am not mad, most noble Sapricius."

"Here, then, is the incense, sacrifice, and save thy life."

"I will not sacrifice," replied Dorothea.

"Then shalt thou die," said Sapricius; and he bade the doomsman take her to the place of execution and strike off her head.

Now as she was being led away from the judgment-seat, a gay young advocate named Theophilus said to her jestingly: "Farewell, sweet Dorothea: when thou hast joined thy lover, wilt thou not send me some of the fruit and roses of his Paradise?"

Looking gravely and gently at him, Dorothea answered: "I will send some."

Whereupon Theophilus laughed merrily, and went his way homeward.

At the place of execution, Dorothea begged the doomsman to tarry a little, and kneeling by the block, she raised her hands to heaven and prayed earnestly. At that moment a fair child stood beside her, holding in his hand a basket containing three golden apples and three red roses.

"Take these to Theophilus, I pray thee," she said to the child, "and tell him Dorothea awaits him in the Paradise whence they came."

Then she bowed her head, and the sword of the doomsman fell.

William Canton

Mark now what follows.

Theophilus, who had reached home, was still telling of what had happened and merrily repeating his jest about the fruit and flowers of Paradise, when suddenly, while he was speaking, the child appeared before him with the apples and the roses. "Dorothea," he said, "has sent me to thee with these, and she awaits thee in the garden." And straightway the child vanished.

The fragrance of those heavenly roses filled Theophilus with a strange pity and gladness; and, eating of the fruit of the Angels, he felt his heart made new within him, so that he, also, became a servant of the Lord Jesus, and suffered death for His name, and thus attained to the celestial garden.

Centuries after her martyrdom, the body of Dorothea was laid in a bronze shrine richly inlaid with gold and jewels in the church built in her honour beyond Tiber, in the seven-hilled city of Rome.

There it lay in the days when Waldo was a brother at the Priory of Three Fountains, among the wooded folds of the Taunus Hills; and every seven years the shrine was opened that the faithful might gaze on the maiden martyr of Caesarea.

An exceeding great love and devotion did Waldo bear this holy virgin, whom he had chosen for his patroness, and one of his most ardent wishes was that he might some day visit the church beyond Tiber, and kneel by the shrine which contained her precious relics. In summer the red roses, in autumn the bright apples on the tree, reminded him of her; in the spring he thought of her youth and beauty joyously surrendered to Christ, and the snow in winter spoke to him of her spotless innocence. Thus through the round of the year the remembrance of her was present about him in fair suggestions; and indeed had there been any lack of these every gift of God would have recalled her to his mind, for was not that—"the gift of God"—her name?

Notwithstanding his youth, Waldo was ripe in learning, well skilled in Latin and Greek, and so gifted beyond measure in poetry and music that people said he had heard the singing of Angels and had brought the echo of it to the earth. His hymns and sacred songs were known and loved all through the German land, and far beyond. The children sang them in the processions on the high feast days, the peasants sang them at their work in house or field, travellers sang them as they journeyed over the long heaths and through the mountain-forests, fishers and raftsmen sang them on the rivers. He composed the Song of the Sickle which cuts at a stroke the corn in its ripeness and the wild flower in its bloom, and the Song of the Mill-wheel, with its long creak and quick clap, and the melodious rush of water from the buckets of the wheel, and many another which it would take long to tell of; but that which to himself was sweetest and dearest was Golden Apples and Roses Red, the song in which he told the legend of St. Dorothea his patroness.

Now when Waldo was in the six-and-thirtieth year of his age he was smitten with leprosy; and when it was found that neither the relics of the saints, nor the prayers of holy men, nor the skill of the physician availed to cure him, but that it was God's will he should endure to the end, the Prior entreated him to surrender himself to that blessed will, and to go forth courageously to the new life of isolation which awaited him. For in those days it was not lawful that a leper should abide in the companionship of men, and he was set apart lest his malady should bring others to a misery like his own.

William Canton

Deep was the grief of the brethren of Three Fountains when they were summoned to attend the sacred office of demission which was to shut out Waldo for ever from intercourse with his fellows. And well might any good heart sorrow, for this was the order of that office.

The altar was draped in black, and Mass for the Dead was sung; and all the things that Waldo would need in the house of his exile, from the flint and iron which gave fire to the harp which should give solace, were solemnly blessed and delivered to him. Next he was warned not to approach the dwellings of men, or to wash in running streams, or to handle the ropes of draw-wells, or to drink from the cups of wayside springs. He was forbidden the highways, and when he went abroad a clapper must give token of his coming and going. Nothing that might be used by others should he touch except with covered hands.

When after these warnings he had been exhorted to patience and trust in God's mercy and love, the brethren formed a procession, with the cross going before, and led him away to his hermitage among the wooded hills. On a little wood-lawn, beyond a brook crossed by stepping-stones, a hut of boughs had been prepared for him, and the Prior bade him mark the grey boulder on the further side of the brook, for there he would find left for him, week by week, such provisions as he needed.

Last rite of all, the Prior entering the hut strewed over his bed of bracken a handful of mould from the churchyard saying, "Sis mortuus mundo—Dead be thou to the world, but living anew to God," and turfs from the churchyard were laid on the roof of the hut. Thus in his grey gown and hood was Waldo committed alive to his grave, and the brethren, chanting a requiem, returned to the Priory.

The tidings of Waldo's grievous lot travelled far and wide through the German land, and thenceforth when his songs were sung many a true man's heart was heavy and many a good woman's eyes were filled with tears as they bethought them of the poor singer in his hut among the hills. Kindly souls brought alms and provisions and laid them on his boulder by the brook, and oftentimes as they came and went they sang some hymn or song he had composed, for they said, "So best can we let him know that we remember him and love him." Indeed, to his gentle heart the sound of their human voices in that solitude was as the warm clasp of a beloved hand.

When Waldo had lived there alone among the hills for the space of two years and more, and his malady had grown exceeding hard to bear, he was seized with a woeful longing—such a longing as comes upon a little child for its mother when it has been left all alone in the house, and has gone seeking her in all the chambers, and finds she is not there. And as on a day he went slowly down to the boulder by the stream in the failing light, thinking of her who had cherished his childhood—how he had clung to her gown, how with his little hand in hers he had run by her side, how she had taken him on her lap and made his hurts all well with kisses, his heart failed him, and crying aloud "Mother, O mother!" he knelt by the boulder, and laid his head on his arms, weeping.

Then from among the trees on the further side of the brook came a maiden running, but she paused at the stepping-stones when she saw Waldo, and said, "Was it thy voice I heard calling 'Mother'?"

The monk did not answer or move.

"Art thou Brother Waldo?" she asked.

William Canton

Raising his head, he looked at her and replied, "I am Brother Waldo."

"Poor brother, I pity thee," said the maiden; "there is no man or maid but pities thee. If thou wilt tell me of thy mother, I will find her, even were I to travel far, and bid her come to thee. Well I wot she will come to thee if she may."

For all his manhood and learning and holiness, Waldo could not still the crying of the little child within him, and he told the maiden of his mother, and blessed her, and asked her name. When she answered that it was Dorothy, "Truly," said he, "it is a fair name and gracious, and in thy coming thou hast been a gift of God to me."

Thereupon the maiden left him, and Waldo returned to his hut, comforted and full of hope.

After a month had gone Dorothy returned. Crossing the stepping-stones in the clear light of the early morning, she found Waldo meditating by the door of his hut.

"I have done thy bidding, brother," she said in a gentle voice, "but alas! thy mother cannot come to thee. Grieve not too much at this, for she is with God. She must have died about the time thou didst call for her; and well may I believe that it was she who sent me to thee in her stead."

"The will of God be done," said Waldo, and he bowed his head, and spoke no more for a long while; but the maiden stood patiently awaiting till he had mastered his grief.

At length he raised his head and saw her. "Art thou not gone?" he asked. "I thought thou hadst gone. Thou art good and gentle, and I thank thee. Go now, for here thou mayst not stay."

"Nay, brother," replied Dorothy, "thou hast no mother to come to thee now, no companion or friend to minister to thee. This is my place. Do not fear that I shall annoy or weary thee. I shall but serve and obey thee, coming and going at thy bidding. Truly thou art too weak and afflicted to be left any more alone."

"It may not be, dear child. Thy father and mother or others of thy kinsfolk need thee at home."

"All these have been long dead," said Dorothy, "and I am alone. Here in the wood I will find me a hollow tree, and thou shalt but call to have me by thee, and but lift a finger to see me no more."

"Why wouldst thou do this for me?" asked Waldo, wondering at her persistency.

"Ah, brother, I know thy suffering and I love thy songs."

"And dost thou not shudder at this horror that is upon me, and dread lest the like befall thee too?"

Then Dorothy laughed low and softly to herself, and answered only so.

In this wise the maiden came to minister to the poor recluse, and so gracious was she and humble, so prudent and yet so tender, that in his suffering she was great solace to him, bringing his food from the boulder and his drink from the brook, cleaning his cell and freshening it with fragrant herbs; and about the cell she made a garden of wholesome plants and wild flowers, and all kindly service that was within her power she did for him.

So beautiful was she and of such exceeding sweetness, that

William Canton

when his eyes rested upon her, he questioned in his mind whether she was a true woman and not an Angel sent down to console him in his dereliction. And that doubt perplexed and troubled him, for so little are we Angels yet that in our aches and sorrows of the flesh it is not the comfort of Angels but the poor human pitiful touch of the fellow-creature that we most yearn for. Once, indeed, he asked her fretfully, "Tell me truly in the name of God, art thou a very woman of flesh and blood?"

"Truly then, brother," she answered, smiling, "I am of mortal flesh and blood even as thou art, and time shall be when this body that thou seest will be mingled with the dust of the earth."

"Is it then the way of women to sacrifice so much for men as thou hast done for me?"

"It is the way of women who love well," said Dorothy.

"Then needs must I thank thy namesake and my patroness in heaven," rejoined Waldo.

"Yea, and is St. Dorothea thy patroness?" asked the maiden.

Waldo told her that so it was, and rapturously he spoke of the young and beautiful saint done to death in Caesarea, and of the fruit and flowers of Paradise which she sent to Theophilus. "And I would," he sighed under his breath, "that she would send such a gift to me."

"All this I know," said Dorothy, "for I have learnt thy song of Golden Apples and Roses Red, and I love it most of all thy songs, though these be many and sung all about the world, I think. And this I will tell thee of thy songs, that I saw in a dream once how they were not mere words and melody, but living things. Like the bright heads of baby Angels were they, and they were carried on wings as it were of rose-leaves, and they fluttered about the people who loved them and sang them, leading them into blessed paths and whispering to them holy and happy thoughts."

"God be blessed and praised for ever, if it be so," said Waldo; "but this was no more than a maiden's dream."

For two winters Dorothy ministered to the poor leper, and during this while no one save Waldo knew of her being in the woods, and no other man set eyes on her. The fourth year of his exile was now drawing to a close, and Waldo had fallen into extreme weakness by reason of his malady, and over his face he wore a mask of grey cloth, with two holes for his great piteous eyes. It was in the springtide, and one night as he lay sleepless in the dark, listening to the long murmur of the wind in the swaying pines, he heard overhead sharp cries and trumpetings, and the creaking and winnowing of wings innumerable.

Rising from his bed, he went out of doors, and looked up into the dark heavens; and high and spectral among the clouded stars he saw the home-coming of the cranes. He sat on the bench beside his door, and watched them sail past in thousands, filling the night with a fleeting clamour and eerie sounds. As he sat he mused on the strange longing which brought these birds over land and sea back home, year by year, with the returning spring, and he marvelled that the souls of men, which are but birds of passage in these earthly fields, should be so slow to feel that longing for their true home-land.

That day when Dorothy came to the hut, he said to her: "It is well to be glad, for, though the air is still keen, the spring is here. I heard the cranes returning in the night."

William Canton

"And I too heard them; and I heard thee rejoicing, playing on thy harp and singing."

"That could not be, sister," said Waldo, "unless in a dream. No longer can I touch harp-string, as thou knowest."

"In truth I was awake and heard," said Dorothy; "and the song thou wast singing was of birds of passage, and of the longing of exiles to go home, and of the dark wherethrough we must pass, with cries and beating wings, ere we can find our way back to our true home-land."

"Nay, it must have been a dream," said Waldo, "for as I sat with my hands hidden in my gown I did but play an imaginary harp, making still music in my heart, and no song came from my lips."

"The more strange that I should hear!" replied Dorothy, smiling as she went her way.

In a little while from this the poor brother felt that the end of his martyrdom drew nigh; and as he lay feeble and faint in the shadow of the hut (for the day was clement), sighing for the hour of his deliverance, Dorothy came from the woods. In her hand she carried a basket, and as she stood over him she said, "See what I have brought for thee."

Lifting his head weakly, and looking through the eyelets of his grey mask, Waldo saw that the basket contained three golden apples and three red roses, though still it was but early days in spring. At sight of them he uttered a cry of gladness (for all it was a cry hollow and hoarse), and strove to rise and throw himself at her feet.

"Nay, brother," she said, "refrain; lie still and breathe the sweetness of the roses and taste of the fruit."

She gave him one of the apples, and putting it to his mouth he tasted it and sighed deeply. In a moment all pain and suffering had left him, and his spirit was light and gladsome. His eyes too were opened, so that he knew that Dorothy had no way deceived him, but was truly a living woman of flesh and blood like himself. Then a heavenly peace descended upon him like a refreshing dew, and he closed his eyes for the great ease he felt.

While these things were happening, came from Three Fountains the lay-brother who brought Waldo his provisions. Crossing the brook to set his budget on the boulder, he saw the poor recluse lying in the lee of the hut, and Dorothy leaning over him. Wherefore he hastened across the wood-lawn, but in an instant the fair woman vanished before his eyes, and when he came to the hut he saw that Waldo was dead. He carried the basket of flowers and fruit to the Priory, and told what he had seen; and the Prior, marvelling greatly, came to the place and gave the poor leper brother a blessed burial.

Now at this time a wondrous strange occurrence was the talk of Rome.

The year wherein Waldo died was that seventh year in which the shrine of St. Dorothea is opened in her church beyond Tiber; and the day on which it is opened fell a little while before the death of Waldo.

Behold, then, when on the vigil of that feast the priests unlocked the shrine, the place where aforetime the holy body of the martyr had lain was empty. Great was the dismay, loud the lamentation, grievous the suspicion. The custodians of the church and the shrine were seized and cast into prison, where they lay till the day of their trial. On the morning of that day the church of St. Dorothea was filled with a divine

William Canton

fragrance, which seemed to transpire from the empty shrine as from a celestial flower. Wherefore once again the shrine was opened, and there, even such as they had been seen by many of the faithful seven years before, lay the relics of the Saint in their old resting-place.

Now to all poor souls God grant a no less happy end of days than this which He vouchsafed to the poor leper-singer Waldo of the Priory of Three Fountains.

THE SEVEN YEARS OF SEEKING

Here begins the chapter of the Seven Years of Seeking.

For, trying greatly to win sight of that blessed isle, the Earthly Paradise, the monk Serapion and his eleven companions hoisted sail; and for seven years they continued in that seeking, wandering with little respite under cloud and star, in all the ways of the sea of ocean which goeth round the world.

[Now this chapter was read of evenings in the refectory at supper, in the winter of the Great Snow. While the drifts without lay fathom-deep in sheltered places, and the snow was settling on the weather-side of things in long slopes like white pent-houses, the community listened with rapt attention, picturing to themselves the slanting ship, and the red sail of skins with its yellow cross in the midst, and the marvellous vision of vast waters, and the strange islands. Then suddenly the Prior would strike the table, and according to the custom the reader would close his book with the words, "Tu autem, Domine—But do Thou, O Lord, have mercy upon us!" and the monks would rise, with interest still keen in the wanderings of the Sea-farers.

Seeing that it would be of little profit to break up the reading as the Prior was wont to break it up, I will give the story here

William Canton

without pause or hindrance, as though it had all been read in a single evening at supper, and keep my "Tu autem" for the end of all. And truly it is at the end of all that most there is need of that prayer. So without more ado.]

Serapion and his companions were, all save one, monks of the Abbey of the Holy Face. Not the first Abbey of that name, in the warm green woods in the western creek of Broce-Liande, but the second, which is nearer to the sunrise. For the site of the first Abbey was most delightful, and so sheltered from the weary wind of the west, and so open to the radiance of the morning, that, save it were Paradise, no man could come at a place so gracious and delectable. There earliest broke the land into leaf and blossom; and there the leaf was last to fall; and there one could not die, not even the very aged. Wherefore, in order that the long years of their pilgrimage might be shortened, the brethren prevailed on the Abbot to remove to another site, nearer the spring of the day; and in this new house, one by one in due season, they were caught up to the repose of the heavens, the aged fathers dying first, as is seemly.

This then was the second Abbey of the Holy Face, and its pleasant woods ran down to the shore of the sea. And going east or going west, where the green billow shades into blue water, the ships of the mariners kept passing and repassing day after day; and their sails seemed to cast an enchanted shadow across the cloister; and the monks, as they watched them leaning over to the breeze, dreamed of the wondrous Garden of Eden, which had not been swallowed up by the Deluge, but had been saved as an isle inviolate amid the fountains of the great deep; and they asked each other whether not one of all these sea-farers would ever bring back a fruit or a flower or a leaf from the arbours of delight in which our first parents had dwelt. They spoke of the voyage of Brendan the Saint, and of the exceeding loveliness of the

Earthly Paradise, and of the deep bliss of breathing its air celestial, till it needed little to set many of them off on a like perilous adventure.

Of all the brethren Serapion was the most eager to begin that seeking. And this was what brought him to it at last.

There came to the Abbey on a day in spring that youthful Bishop of Arimathea who in after time made such great fame in the world. Tall and stately was he, and black-bearded; a guest pleasant and wise, and ripe with the experience of distant travel and converse with many chief men. Now he was on his way to the great house of Glastonbury oversea, to bring back with him, if he might be so fortunate, the body of the saint of his city who had helped our Lord to bear His cross on the Way Dolorous; or, if that were an issue beyond his skill, at least some precious memorial of that saint.

Many things worthy of remembrance he told of what he had seen and heard; and no small marvel did it seem to speak with one who had stood on Mount Sinai in the wilderness. From the top of that mountain, he said, one looked down on a region stretching to the Red Sea, and in the midst of the plain there is a monastery of saintly recluses, but no man can discover any track that leads to it. Faint and far away the bells are heard tolling for prime, it may be, or vespers, and it is believed that now and again some weary traveller has reached it, but no one has ever returned. The Ishmaelites, who dwell in the wilderness, have ridden long in search of it, guided by the sound of the bells, but never have they succeeded in catching a gleam of its white walls among the palm-trees, nor yet of the green palms. The Abbot of that house, it is said, is none other than the little child whom our Lord set in the midst of His Disciples, saying, "Except ye become as little children," and he will abide on the earth till our Lord's return, and then shall he enter into the kingdom with Him, without tasting death.

Speaking of the holy places, Calvary, it might be, or the Garden of Olives and the sepulchre of the Lord, and of the pilgrims who visited these, he repeated to us the saying of the saintly Father Hieronymus: "To live in Jerusalem is not a very holy thing, but to live a holy life in Jerusalem." And walking with many of our brethren on the shore of the sea and seeing the sails of the ships as they went by, he questioned us of the wonders of the great waters, and of sea-faring, and of the last edge of the living earth, and he said: "Tell me, you who abide within sight of so many ships, and who hear continually the song of the great creature Sea, how would it fare with one who should sail westward and keep that one course constantly?"

We said that we knew not; it were like he would perish of famine or thirst, or be whelmed in the deep.

"Ay," he said, "but if he were well provisioned, with no lack of food and water, and the weather held fair?"

That we could not answer, for it seemed to us that such a one would lose heart and hope in the roofless waste, with never a stone or tree, nor any shadow save a cloud's, and turn back dismayed; but Serapion replied: "To me it appears, your Discretion, that so bold a mariner, if years failed him not, might win to the Earthly Paradise."

"So have I heard," said the Bishop. "Yet here would you be sailing into the west, and for a certainty the Paradise of God was in the east. How would you give a reasonable account of this?"

But we could make no reply, for we knew not; nor Serapion more than we.

"Now, watching the sea," said the Bishop, "you have marked the ships, how they go. When they come to you, they first show the mast-top, then the sail, and last the body of the ship, and perchance the sweep of the oars, reverse-wise when they depart from you, you first fail to see the body of the ship, and then the sail, but longest you hold in sight the mast-top, or it may be a bright streamer flying therefrom, or a cross glittering in the light—though these be but small things compared with the body of the ship. Is it not so?"

We answered, readily enough, that so it was.

"Is it not then even as though one were to watch a wayfarer on horse-back, going or coming over the green bulge of a low hill? Were he coming to you, you would first see the head of the rider, and last the legs of the horse, and were he riding away the horse would first go down over the hill, but still, for a little, you would see the man waving his hand in farewell as he sank lower and lower."

Such indeed, we said, was the fashion of a ship's coming and going.

"Does it not then seem a likely thing," said his Discretion, "that the sea is in the nature of a long low hill, down which the ships go? So have I heard it surmised by wise men, sages and scholars of the lights of heaven, in the cities of Greece and Egypt. For the earth and the ocean-sea, they teach, is fashioned as a vast globe in the heights of heaven. And truly, if indeed it be the shadow of the world which darkens the face of the moon in time of eclipse, the earth may well be round, for that shadow is round. Thus, then, one holding ever a westward course might sail down the bulge of the sea, and under the world, and round about even unto the east, if there be sea-way all along that course."

William Canton

Silently we listened to so strange a matter, but the Bishop traced for us on the sand a figure of the earth. "And here," said he, "is this land of ours, and here the sea, and here the bulge of ocean, and here a ship sailing westward; and here in the east is the Earthly Paradise; and mark now how the ship fareth onward ever on the one course unchanged, till it cometh to that blessed place."

Truly this was a wondrous teaching; and when we questioned how they who sailed could escape falling out and perishing, they and indeed their ship, when they came so far down the round sea that they hung heads nethermost, his Discretion laughed: "Nay, if the sea, which the wind breaketh and lifteth and bloweth about in grey showers, fall not out, neither will the ship, nor yet the mariners; for the Lord God hath so ordered it that wheresoever mariners be, there the sea shall seem to them no less flat than a great grass-meadow when the wind swings the grass; and if they hang head downward they know not of it; but rather, seeing over them the sun and the clouds, they might well pity our evil case, deeming it was we who were hanging heads nethermost."

Now this and suchlike converse with the Bishop so moved Serapion that he lost the quietude of soul and the deep gladness of heart which are the portion of the cloister. Day and night his thought was flying under sail across the sea towards the Earthly Paradise, and others there were who were of one longing with him. Wherefore at last they prayed leave of the Abbot to build a ship and to try the venture.

The Abbot consented, but when they besought him to go with them and to lead them, he shook his head smiling, and answered: "Nay, children, I am an aged man, little fitted for such a labour. Wiser is it for me to lean my staff against my fig-tree, and have in mind the eternal years. Moreover, as you know, many are the sons in this house who look to me for fatherly care. But if it be your wish, one shall go with you to be the twelfth of your company. In hours of peril and perplexity and need, if such should befall you, you shall bid him pray earnestly, and after he has prayed, heed what he shall say, even as you would heed the words of your Abbot. No better Abbot and counsellor could you have, for he hath still preserved his baptismal innocence. It is Ambrose, the little chorister."

Serapion and the others wondered at this, but readily they accepted the Abbot's choice of a companion.

Think now of the ship as built—a goodly ship of stout timber frame covered two-ply with hides seasoned and sea-worthy, well found in provisions against a long voyage, fitted with sturdy mast of pine and broad sail. And think of the Mass as sung, with special prayer to Him who is the confidence of them that are afar off upon the sea. And think of the leave-taking and blessing as over and done, and of the Sea-farers as all aboard, eleven brethren and Ambrose the chorister, a little lad of nine summers.

Now all is cast loose, and the red sail is drawn up the mast and set puffing, and the ship goes out, dipping and springing, into the deep. On the shore the religious stand watching; and Serapion is at the rudder, steering and glancing back; and the others aboard are waving hands landward; and on a thwart beside the mast stands the little lad, and at a sign from Serapion he lifts up his clear sweet voice, singing joyfully the *Kyrie eleison* of the Litany. The eleven join in the glad song, and it is caught up by the voices of those on shore, as though it were by an organ; and as he sings the lad Ambrose watches the white ruffled wake-water of the ship, how it streams between the unbroken green sea on either hand, and it seems to him most like the running of a shallow brook

William Canton

when it goes ruffling over the pebbles in the greenwood.

To those on ship and to those on shore the song of each grew a fainter hearing as the distance widened; and the magnitude of the ship lessened; and first the hull went down the bulge of the ocean, and next the sail; and long ere it was sunset all trace of the Sea-farers had vanished away.

Now is this company of twelve gone forth into the great waters; far from the beloved house of the Holy Face are they gone, and far from the blithesome green aspect of the good earth; and no man of them knoweth what bane or blessing is in store for him, or whether he shall ever again tread on grass or ground. A little tearfully they think of their dear cloister-mates, but they are high of heart nothing the less. Their ship is their garth, and cloister, and choir, wherein they praise God with full voices through all the hours from matins to compline.

Of the bright weather and fresh wind which carried them westward many days it would be tedious to tell, and indeed little that was strange did they see at that time, save it were a small bird flying high athwart their course, and a tree, with its branches and green leaves unlopped, which lay in the swing of the wave; but whither and whence the bird was flying, or where that tree grew in soil, they could not guess.

Of what happened to them in the course of their seeking, even of that the telling must be brief, flitting from one event to another, even as the small Peter-bird flits from the top of one wave to the top of another, nor wets foot or feather in the marbled sea between; else would the story of the seeking linger out the full seven years of the seeking.

The first trial that befell them was dense wintry fog, in the dusk of which they lay with lowered sail on a sullen sea for a day and a night. When the change came, it brought with it the blowing of a fierce gale with a plague of sleet and hailstones, and they were chased out of the fog, and driven far into the south.

Great billows followed them as they ran, and broke about the stern of the ship in fountains of freezing spray which drenched them to the skin. Little ease had they in their seafaring in that long race with the north wind, for every moment they looked to have the mast torn up by the root and the frame-work of the ship broken asunder. The salt surf quenched their fire and mingled their bread with bitterness.

Aching they were and weary, and sorrowful enough to sleep, when the tempest abated, and the sun returned, and the sea rolled in long glassy swells.

As the sun blazed out, and the sea glittered over all his trackless ways, Serapion said to the chorister: "Ha, little brother, 'tis good, is it not? to see the bright sun once more. His face is as the face of an Angel to us."

The lad looked at him curiously, but made no answer.

"Art thou ailing, or sad, or home-sick, little one, that thou hast nought to say?" asked Serapion.

"Nay, father, I was but thinking of thy words, that the face of the sun is as the face of an Angel."

"Ay! And is it not so?"

"Nay, father. When I have seen the sun at sunrise and at sunset I have ever seen a ring of splendid Angels, and in the midst of the ring the snow-white Lamb with his red cross, and the Angels were moving constantly around the Lamb, joyfully glittering; and that was the sun. But as it rose into the heavens the Angels dazzled mine eyes so that I could see them no more, nor yet the Lamb, for very brightness. Is the sun then otherwise than what I see?"

Then was it Serapion's turn to muse, and he answered:

"To thy young eyes which be clear and strong—yet try them not overmuch—it is doubtless as thou sayest; but we who are older have lost the piercing sight, and to us the sun is but a great and wonderful splendour which dazzles us before we can descry either the Angels or the Lamb."

Meanwhile the Sea-farers ate and drank and spread their raiment to dry, and some were oppressed by the memory of the hardships they had endured; but Serapion, going among them, cheered them with talk of the Earthly Paradise, and of the joy it would be, when they had won thither, to think of the evil chances through which they had passed. In a low tone he also spoke to them of their small companion and his vision of the sun.

"Truly," he said, "it is as our Father Abbot told us—he has not lost his baptismal innocence, nor hath he lost all knowledge of the heaven from which he came."

As he was speaking thus, one of the brethren rose up with a cry, and, shading his eyes with his hand, pointed into the west. Far away in the shimmer of the sea and the clouds they perceived an outline of land, and they changed their course a little to come to it. The wind carried them bravely on, and they began to distinguish blue rounded hills and ridges, and a little later green woodland, and still later, on the edge of twilight, the white gleam of waters, and glimpses of open lawns tinged with the colour of grasses in flower.

With beating hearts they leaned on the low bulwark of the ship, drinking in the beauty of the island.

Then out of a leafy creek shot a boat of white and gold; and though it was far off, the air was so crystalline that they saw it was garlanded with fresh leaves, and red and yellow and blue blossoms; and in it there were many lovely forms, clothed in white and crowned with wreaths rose-coloured and golden.

When the Sea-farers perceived that the boat glided towards them without sail or oar, they said among themselves, "These are assuredly the spirits of the Blessed;" and when suddenly the boat paused in its course, and the islanders began a sweet song, and the brethren caught the words and knew them for Latin, they were fain to believe that they had, by special grace and after brief tribulations, got within sight of the shore they sought.

The song was one of a longing for peace and deep sleep and dreamful joy and love in the valleys of the isle; and it bade the Sea-farers come to them, and take repose after cold and hunger and toil on the sea. Tears of gladness ran down the cheeks of several of the Seekers as they listened, and one of them cried aloud: "O brothers, we have come far, but it is worth the danger and the suffering to hear this welcome of the Blessed."

Now the small chorister, who was standing by Serapion at the helm, touched the father's sleeve, and asked in a low voice: "Have I leave to sing in answer?"

"Sing, little son," Serapion replied.

Then, ringing the blessed bell of the Sea-farers, the child intoned the evening hymn:

William Canton

Te lucis ante terminum—
Before the waning of the light.

The instant his fresh young voice was heard singing that holy hymn, the flower-garlands about the boat broke into ghastly flames, and wreathed it with a dreadful burning; and the radiant figures were changed into dark shapes crowned with fire; and the song of longing and love became a wailing and gnashing of teeth. The island vanished away in rolling smoke; and the boat burned down like a darkening ember; and the Sea-farers in their ship were once more alone in the wilderness of waters.

Long they prayed that night, praising God that they had escaped the snares and enchantments of the fiends. And Serapion, drawing the lad to him, kissed him, saying: "God be with thee, little brother, in thy uprising and thy down-lying! God be with thee, little son!"

After this they were again driven into the south for many a day, and saw no earthly shore, but everywhere unending waters. A great wonderment to them was this immensity of the sea of ocean, wherein the land seemed a little thing lost for ever. And ever as they drove onward, the pilot star of the north was steadfast no longer, but sank lower and still lower in the heavens, and many of the everlasting lights, which at home they had seen swing round it through the livelong night, were now sunken, as it were, in the billows.

"Truly," said Serapion, "it is even as his Discretion the Bishop told us; whether east we sail or west, or cross-wise north and south, the earth is of the figure of a ball. In a little while it may be that we shall see the pilot star no more;" and he was sorely troubled in his mind as to how they should steer thereafter with no beacon in heaven to guide them, and how they would make their way back to the Abbey of the

Holy Face.

In their wandering they set eyes on a thing well-nigh incredible—nothing less than fishes rising from the depths of the sea, and flying like birds over the ship, and diving into the sea again, and yet again rising into the air and disporting themselves in the sun. At night, too, they beheld about the ship trails of fire in the sea, crossing and re-crossing each other, and the fire marked the ways of huge blue fishes, swift and terrible; and the Sea-farers prayed that these malignant searchers of the deep might not rise into the air and fall ravening upon them while they slept. In the darkness strange patches and tangles of light, blue and golden and emerald, floated past them, and these they discovered were living creatures to which they could give no names. Often also the sea was alive with fire, which flashed and ran along the ridges of the waves when they curled and broke, and many a night the sides of the ship were washed with flame, but this fire was wet and cold, and nowise hurt a hand of those who touched it.

At last on a clear morning the little chorister came hastily to Serapion and said: "Look, father, is not yon a glimmer of the heavenly land we seek?"

"Nay, little son, it is but grey cloud that has not yet caught the sun," replied Serapion.

"That, indeed, is cloud; but look higher, father. See how white and sharp it shines!"

Then Serapion lifted up his eyes above the cloud, and in mid heaven there floated as it were a great rock of pointed crystal, white and unearthly. Serapion's eyes brightened with eagerness, and the Sea-farers gazed long at the peak, which rather seemed a star, or a headland on some celestial shore, so bright and dreamlike was it and so magically poised in the high air.

All day they sailed towards it, and sometimes it vanished from their view, but it returned constantly. On the third day they came to that land. Bright and beautiful it was to their sea-wearied eyes; and of a surety no land is there that goes so nearly to heaven. For it rose in green and flowery heights till it was lost in a ring of dusky sea-cloud; and through this vast ring of cloud it pierced its way, and the Sea-farers saw it emerge and stand clear above the cloud, bluish with the distance. And higher still it rose, and entered a second great cloud-ring, but this ring was white; and once more it emerged from the cloud-ring, and high over all towered the pyramid of shining stone.

"Well might it be that Angels often alight on this soaring mountain," said Serapion, "and leave it glittering with their footprints. If life and strength be given us, thither we also shall climb, and praise God in the lofty places of the earth which He has made."

They steered the ship into a sunny bay, and Serapion having blessed the sea and the shore, they landed right joyfully. Drawing the ship high on the beach, they chose a little grove of palm-trees beside a shallow stream for their church and cloister; but they had not been long in that spot before they saw the islanders gliding through the wood and peering out at them in great amaze. Serapion went forth to them, smiling and beckoning them to approach, but they fled and would not abide his coming. So Serapion returned, and the Sea-farers made themselves such a home as they might, and rested a little from their toiling.

When the day had come to evening, and the brethren were chanting vespers, the islanders returned, many hundreds of them, men and women, dusky of skin but comely and bright-eyed, and for all their raiment they wore garlands of blossoms and girdles of woven leaves. Close they came to the Sea-farers, and gazed at them, and the boldest touched them, as though to assure themselves that these were living mortals like unto themselves. But when they saw the little chorister, with his fair white face and childish blue eyes and sunny hair, they turned to each other with exclamations and uncouth gestures of pleasure and wonderment. Then they hurried away and brought strange and delightful fruit—berries, and fruit in a skin yellow and curved like a sickle moon, and big nuts full of water sweet and cool, and these they laid before the lad. Wreaths of flowers, too, they wove for him, and put them on his head and about his neck, as though they were rejoiced to see him and could not make too much of him. The brethren were light of heart that they had come to an isle so gracious and a folk so simple and loving.

Sleep, sweet as dews of Paradise, fell upon their weariness that night, and they rose refreshed and glad for matins, which they chanted by the light of large and radiant stars flashing down through the palms. What happened that day, however, the Sea-farers did not wholly understand till long afterwards, when they had learned the speech of the people; but out of their later knowledge I shall here make it plain.

Now in the olden time the mighty mountain of this island had been a burning mountain, and even now, in a huge craggy cup beneath the glittering peak, there was a vast well of fire and molten rock; and the peak and well were the lair of an evil spirit so strong and terrible that each year the island folk gave him a child to appease him, lest in his malignant mood he should let the well overflow and consume them with its waters of fire.

Wherefore, as this was the season of the sacrifice, the

William Canton

islanders seeing the little chorister, how fair and beautiful he was, deemed he would be a more acceptable offering to the spirit of evil than one of their children, whom they were heart-sick of slaying. On this day, therefore, they came at dawn, and with many gestures and much strange speech led away the lad, and with gentle force kept the brethren apart from him, though they suffered them to follow.

In a little while the child was clothed with flowers and leaves like one of themselves, and in the midst of a great crowd singing a barbarous strain, he was borne on a litter of boughs up the ascent of the mountain. Many times they paused and rested in the heat, and the day was far spent when they reached the foot of the lofty peak. There they passed the night, but though the brethren strove to force their way to the lad, they were restrained by the strength of the multitude, and they knew that violence was useless. Again in the twilight before dawn the islanders resumed the journey and came to the edge of the craggy cup, in the depths of which bubbled the well of fire.

Silently they stood on the brink, looking towards the east; but the Sea-farers, who now deemed only too well that their little brother was about to be sacrificed to Moloch, cast themselves on their knees, and with tears running down their faces, raised their hands in supplication to heaven. But with a loud voice Serapion cried: "Fear not, dear son; for the Lord can save thee from the mouth of the lion, and hear thee from the horns of the unicorns." The little chorister answered: "Pray for my soul, Father Serapion; for my body I have no fear, even though they cast me into the pit."

In the streaming east the rays of light were springing ever more brilliantly over the clear sea; two strong men held the lad and lifted him from the ground; an aged islander—a priest, it seemed, of that evil spirit—white-haired and crowned with flowers, watched the sky with dull eyes; and as the sun came up with a rush of splendour, he called aloud: "God of the mountain-fire, take this life we give thee, and be good and friendly to us."

Then was little Ambrose the chorister swung twice to and fro, and hurled far out into the rocky cup of the well of fire. And a wild cry arose from the crowd: "Take this life, take this life!"—but even as that cry was being uttered the lad was stayed in his fall, and he stood on the air over the fiery well, as though the air had been turned to solid crystal, and he ran on the air across the abyss to the brethren, and Serapion caught him in his arms and folded him to his breast.

Then fell a deep stillness and dread upon the people, and what to do they knew not; but the aged priest and the strong men who had flung the boy into the gulf came to the brethren, and casting themselves on their faces before the chorister, placed his foot on their heads. Wherefore Serapion surmised that they now took him for a youthful god or spirit more powerful than the evil spirit of the fire. Touching them, he signed to them to arise, and when they stood erect he pointed to the abyss, and gathering a handful of dust he threw it despitefully into the well of fire, and afterwards spat into the depths. This show of scorn and contumely greatly overawed the people, and (as was made known afterwards) they looked on the Sea-farers as strong gods, merciful and much to be loved.

Thrice did the Sea-farers hold Easter in that island, for there they resolved to stay till they had learned the island speech, and freed the people from the bondage of demons, and taught them the worship of the one God who is in the heavens.

Now though the wind blew with an icy mouth on that high peak, in the rocks of the crater it was sheltered, and warm

William Canton

because of the inner fires of the mountain. So it was ordered that in turn one brother should abide on the peak, and one in a cave midway down the mountain, and one on the slopes where the palms and orange-trees are rooted among the white-flowered sweet-scented broom. And each of these had a great trumpet of bark, and when the first ray of light streamed out of the east in the new day, the brother of the peak cried through his trumpet with a mighty voice:

Laudetur Jesus Christus,
May Christ Jesus be praised,

and the brother of the cave, having responded,

In saecula saeculorum,
World without end,

cried mightily to the brother of the palms, "May Christ Jesus be praised!"—and thus from the heights in the heavens to the shore of the sea. So, too, when the last light of the setting sun burned out on the western billows.

Thus was the reign of the spirit of evil abolished, and the mountain consecrated to the praise of Him who made the hills and the isles of the sea.

In the strong light of the morning sun the shadow of that mountain is cast over the great sea of ocean further than a swift ship may sail with a fair wind in two days and two nights; and a man placed on the peak shall see that shadow suddenly rise up from the sea and stand over against the mountain, dark and menaceful, like the lost soul of a mountain bearing testimony against its body before the judgment-seat of God; and this is a very awful sight.

Now, having preached the Gospel, the Sea-farers

strengthened their ship and launched into the deep after the third Eastertide, and having comforted the people, because they were grieved and mournful at their departure, they left them in the keeping of the risen Lord, and continued their seeking.

After this Brother Benedict, the oldest monk of their company, fell ill with grievous sickness, and sorely the Sea-farers longed for some shore where he might feel the good earth solid and at rest beneath him, and see the green of growing things, and have the comfort of stillness and silence.

With astonishing patience he bore his malady, at no time repining, and speaking never a word of complaint. When he was asked if he repented him of the adventure, he smiled gently. "Fain, indeed," he said, "would I be laid to rest beneath the grass of our own garth, where the dear brethren, passing and repassing in the cloister, might look where I lay and say an 'Our Father' for my soul. Yet in no way do I repent of our sailing, for we have seen the marvellous works of God; and if the Lord vouchsafe to be merciful to me, it may be that I shall see the Heavenly Paradise before you find the Earthly." "God grant it, dear brother," said Serapion.

On an afternoon they came to a small island walled about with high cliffs, red and brown, and at the foot of the cliffs a narrow beach of ruddy sand; but on the rocks grew no green thing, lichen or moss or grass or shrub, and no sweet water came bickering down into the sea.

On landing they discovered a gully in the cliffs which led inland, and straightway explorers were sent to spy what manner of land it was whereon they had fallen. Within the very mouth of the narrow pass they came upon a small ship hollowed out of a tree gigantic, but it was rotten and dry as touchwood, and wasting into dust. Within the ship lay the

William Canton

bones of a man, stretched out as though he had died in sleep. Outside the ship lay the bones of two others. The faces of these were turned downward to the stones whereon they lay, but the man in the ship had perished with his eyes fixed on the heavens. The oars and sails and ropes were all dry and crumbling, and the raiment of the men had mouldered away.

In the length of that narrow pass between the lofty cliff-walls the Sea-farers found no vestige of grass or weed, either on the cliff-sides or on the stones and shingle. Neither was there any water, save where in the hollows of some of the boulders rain had lodged and had not yet been drunk up by the sun. No living creature, great or small, lived in that ghyll.

Within the round of the sea-walls the island lay flat and low, and it was one bleak waste of boulder and shingle, lifeless and waterless save for the rain in the pitted surfaces of the stones; but in the midst of the waste there stood, dead and leafless, a vast gaunt tree, which at one time must have been a goodly show. When the Sea-farers reached it, they found lying on the dead turf about its roots the white bones of yet four other men.

Much they questioned and conjectured whence these ill-starred wanderers had come to lay their bones on so uncharitable a soil, and whether they had perished in seeking, like themselves, for the Earthly Paradise. "What," sighed one, "if this were the Earthly Paradise, and yon the Tree of Life!" But the others murmured and would not have it so.

Yet to the sick man even this Isle of the Stones of Emptiness was a place of rest and respite from the sea,—"It is still mother-earth," he said, "though the mother be grown very old and there be no flesh left on her bones"—and at first it seemed as though he was recovering in the motionless stillness and in the great shadow of the cliffs. Something of this Serapion said to the little chorister, but the lad answered: "Nay, father, do you not see how the man that used to look out of his eyes has become a very little child—and of such is the kingdom of heaven?"

"Explain, little brother," said Serapion.

"Why," said the lad, "is it not thus with men when they grow so old or sick that they be like to die—does one not see that the real selves within them look out of window with faces grown younger and smaller and more joyous, till it may be that what was once a strong man, wise and great, is but a babbling babe which can scarce walk at all?"

"Who told thee these things?" asked Serapion.

"No one has told me," replied the lad, "but seeing the little children thus gazing out, and knowing that all who would enter into heaven must become as they are, I thought it must needs be in this manner that people change and pass away to God when the ending of life is come."

On this isle the Sea-farers kept a Christmas, and they made such cheer as they might at that blessed time, speaking of the stony fields wherein the Shepherds lay about their flocks, but no fields were ever so stony as these which were littered with stones fathom-deep, with never a grain of earth or blade of grass between. And in this isle it was that Brother Benedict died, very peaceful, and without pain at the close. On the feast of the Three Kings that poor monk was privileged even more than those Kings had been, for not only was the Babe of Heaven made manifest to him, but his soul, a little child, went forth from him to be with that benign Babe for evermore. Under the dead tree the Sea-farers buried him, and on the trunk of the tree they fastened a crucifix on the side on which he reposed.

The bones, too, of the dead men they gathered together and covered with stones in a hollow which they made.

So they left the island, marvelling whence all those stones had come, and how they had been rained many and deep on that one place. Said one, "It may be that these are the stones wherewith our Lord and the prophets and the blessed martyrs were stoned, laid up as in a treasury to bear witness on the day of doom." "It may be," said another, "that these are the stones which Satan, tempting the Lord, bade Him turn into bread, and therefore are they kept for an evidence against the tempter." "Peradventure these be the stony places," said another, "whereon the good seed fell and perished in its first upspringing, and so they be kept for the admonishment of rash Sea-farers and such as have no long-continuance in well-doing." But no man among them was satisfied as to the mystery of that strange isle.

On many other shores they set foot. Most were fruitful and friendly; and they rested from their seeking, and repaired the ship, and took in such stores as they might gather during their sojourn. Though often it befell that while they were still afar the wind wafted them the fragrance of rare spices so that their eyes brightened and their faces reddened with joyful anticipation, yet ever when they landed they found that not yet, not yet had they reached the island garden of their quest. Men, too, of the same fashion as themselves they met with on shores far apart, but strange were these of aspect and speech and manner of life. With them they tarried as long as they might, gaining some knowledge of their tongue, and revealing to them the true God and the Lord crucified.

In the latter time of their sea-faring they were blown far over the northern side of the great sea, in such wise that the pilot star burned well-nigh overhead in the heavens. Here they descried tall islands of glittering rock, white and blue, crowned with minsters and castles and abbeys of glass, but they heard no sound of bells or of men's voices or of the stir of life.

Once as they were swept along in near peril of wreck, through flying sea-smoke and plagues of hail, they heard a strange unearthly music rising and falling in the blast. Some said it was Angels sent to strengthen them; others said it was wild birds which they had seen flying past in flocks; but Serapion said, "If it be Angels, blessed be God; if it be birds, yet even they are God's Angels, lessoning us how we shall praise Him, and sing Him a new song from the ends of the earth." Then he raised his voice, singing the psalm

Laudate Dominum de caelis,
Praise ye the Lord from the heavens:
praise Him in the heights,

and the Sea-farers sang it with earnest voices and with hearts lifted up, and they were greatly encouraged.

It was in these latitudes stormy and cold that, to their thinking, the Sea-farers won nearest to the Earthly Paradise. For, far in the sides of the north as, in the red sunlight, they coasted a lofty land white with snow-fields and blue with glacier ice, they entered a winding fjord, and found themselves in glassy water slumbering between green slopes of summer.

Down to the water's edge the shores were wooded with copses of dwarf birch and willow, and the slopes were radiant with wild flowers—harebell and yellow crowfoot, purple heath and pink azalea and starry saxifrage. A rosy light tinged the snow on the wintry heights; and over the edge of a cliff, far up the fjord, a glacier hung, and from beneath the ice a jet of water burst forth and fell foaming

William Canton

down the precipice to the shore. When they landed they found the ground covered thick with berries dark and luscious, and while they gathered these, a black and white snow-bunting flitted about them on its long wings.

A miraculous thing was this garden of summer in the icy bosom of winter, but a greater marvel still was the undying sunshine on sea and shore.

"In very truth," said Serapion, "of all places we have yet seen is not this most like to have been the blessed land, for is not even 'the night light about us,' and is it not with us as it is written of the Heavenly Jerusalem, 'there shall be no night there'?"

The Sea-farers took away with them many of the leaves and flowers of this country, and afterwards the scribes in the Scriptorium copied them in beautiful colours in the Golden Missal of the Abbey.

This was the last of the unknown shores visited by the Sea-farers. Seven years had they pursued their seeking, and there now grew on them so strong a craving for home that they could gainsay it no longer. Wherefore it fell out that in the autumn-tide, when the stubble is brown in the fields and the apple red on the bough; on the last day of the week, when toil comes to end; in the last light of the day, when the smoke curls up from the roof, they won their long sea-way home.

O beloved Abbey of the Holy Face, through tears they beheld thy walls, with rapture they kissed thy threshold!

"In all the great sea of ocean," said Serapion, when he had told the story of their wandering, "no such Earthly Paradise have we seen as this dear Abbey of our own!"

"Dear brethren," said the Abbot, "the seven years of your seeking have not been wasted if you have truly learned so much. Far from home have I never gone, but many things have come to me. To be ever, and to be tranquilly, and to be joyously, and to be strenuously, and to be thankfully and humbly at one with the blessed will of God—that is the Heavenly Paradise; and each of us, by God's grace, may have that within him. And whoso hath within him the Heavenly Paradise, hath here and now, and at all times and in every place, the true Earthly Paradise round about him."

Here ends the chapter of the Seven Years of Seeking.

["But do Thou, O Lord, have mercy upon us," chanted the Lector, as he closed the book. And the Prior struck the board, and the brethren arose and returned God thanks for the creatures of food and drink, and for that Earthly Paradise, ever at their door, of tranquil and joyous and strenuous and thankful and humble acceptance of God's will.]

William Canton

THE GUARDIANS OF THE DOOR

There was once an orphan girl, far away in a little village on the edge of the moors. She lived in a hovel thatched with reeds, and this was the poorest and the last of all the houses, and stood quite by itself among broom and whins by the wayside.

From the doorway the girl could look across the wild stretches of the moorland; and that was pleasant enough on a summer day, for then the air is clear and golden, and the moor is purple with the bloom of the ling, and there are red and yellow patches of bracken, and here and there a rowan tree grows among the big grey boulders with clusters of reddening berries. But at night, and especially on a winter night, the darkness was so wide and so lonely that it was hard not to feel afraid sometimes. The wind, when it blew in the dark, was full of strange and mournful voices; and when there was no wind, Mary could hear the cries and calls of the wild creatures on the moor.

Mary was fourteen when she lost her father. He was a rough idle good-for-nothing, and one stormy night on his way home from the tavern he went astray and was found dead in the snow. Her mother had died when she was so small a child that Mary could scarcely remember her face. So it happened that she was left alone in the world, and all she possessed was a dog, some fowls, and her mother's spinning wheel.

But she was a bright, cheerful, courageous child, and soon she got from the people of the village sufficient work to keep her wheel always busy, for no one could look into her face without liking her. People often wondered how so rude and worthless a fellow could have had such a child; she was as sweet and unexpected as the white flowers on the bare and rugged branches of the blackthorn.

Her hens laid well, and she sold all the eggs she could spare; and her dog, which had been trained in all sorts of cunning by her father, often brought her from the moors some wild thing in fur or feathers which Mary thought there was no harm in cooking.

Her father had been too idle and careless to teach her anything, and all that she could recollect of her mother's instruction was a little rhyme which she used to repeat on her knees beside the bed every night before she went to sleep.

And this was the rhyme:

God bless this house from thatch to floor,
The twelve Apostles guard the door,
And four good Angels watch my bed,
Two at the foot and two the head.

Amen.

Though she was all alone in the world, and had no girl of her own age to make friends with, she was happy and contented, for she was busy from morning till night.

And yet in spite of all this, strange stories began to be

whispered about the village. People who happened to pass by the old hut late at night declared that they had seen light shining through the chinks in the window-shutter when all honest people should have been asleep. There were others who said they had noticed strange men standing in the shadows of the eaves; they might have been highwaymen, they might have been smugglers—they could not tell, for no one had cared to run the risk of going too near—but it was quite certain that there were strange things going on at the hut, and that the girl who seemed so simple and innocent was not quite so good as the neighbours had imagined.

When the village gossip had reached the ears of the white-headed old Vicar, he sent for the girl and questioned her closely. Mary was grieved to learn that such untrue and unkind stories were told about her. She knew nothing, she said, of any lights or of any men. As soon as it was too dusky to see to work she always fastened her door, and after she had had her supper, she covered the fire and blew out the rushlight and went to bed.

"And you say your prayers, my daughter, I hope?" said the Vicar kindly.

Mary hung down her head and answered in a low voice, "I do not know any proper prayers, but I always say the words my mother taught me."

And Mary repeated the rhyme:

God bless this house from thatch to floor,
The twelve Apostles guard the door,
And four good Angels watch my bed,
Two at the foot and two the head.

Amen.

"There could not be a better prayer, dear child!" rejoined the Vicar, with a smile. "Go home now, and do not be troubled by what idle tongues may say. Every night repeat your little prayer, and God will take care of you."

Late that night, however, the Vicar lit his lantern and went out of doors, without a word to any one. All the village was still and dark as he walked slowly up the road towards the moor.

"She is a good girl," he said to himself, "but people may have observed something which has given rise to these stories. I will go and see with my own eyes."

The stars were shining far away in the dark sky, and the green plovers were crying mournfully on the dark moor. As he passed along the lantern swung out a dim light across the road, which had neither walls nor hedges.

"It is a lonely place for a child to live in by herself," he thought.

At last he perceived the outline of the old hovel, among the gorse and broom, and the next moment he stopped suddenly, for there, as he had been told, a thread of bright light came streaming through the shutters of the small window. He drew his lantern under his cloak, and approached cautiously. The road where he stood was now dim, but by the faint glimmer of the stars he was able to make out that there were several persons standing under the eaves, and apparently whispering together.

The Vicar's good old heart was filled with surprise and sorrow. Then it suddenly grew hot with anger, and throwing aside his cloak and lifting up the lantern he advanced boldly to confront the intruders. But they were not at all alarmed,

William Canton

and they did not make any attempt to escape him. Then, as the light fell upon their forms and faces, who but the Vicar was struck with awe and amazement, and stood gazing as still as a stone!

The people under the eaves were men of another age and another world, strangely clothed in long garments, and majestic in appearance. One carried a lance, and another a pilgrim's staff, and a third a battle-axe; but the most imposing stood near the door of the hut, and in his hand he held two large keys.

In an instant the Vicar had guessed who they were, and had uncovered his head and fallen on his knees; but the strangers melted slowly away into the darkness, as if they had been no more than the images of a dream. And indeed the Vicar might have thought that he really had been dreaming but for the light which continued to stream through the chink in the shutter.

He arose from his knees and moved towards the window to peep into the hut. Instantly an invisible hand stretched a naked sword across his path, and a low deep voice spoke to him in solemn warning:

"It is the light of Angels. Do not look, or blindness will fall upon you, even as it fell upon me on the Damascus road."

But the aged Vicar laid his hand on the sword, and tried to move it away.

"Let me look, let me look!" he said; "better one glimpse of the Angels than a thousand years of earthly sight."

Then the sword yielded to his touch and vanished into air, and the old priest leaned forward on the window-sill and gazed through the chink. And with a cry of joy he saw a corner of the rude bed, and beside the corner, one above the other, three great dazzling wings; they were the left-hand side wings of one of the Angels at the foot of the bed.

Then all was deep darkness.

The Vicar thought that it was the blindness that had fallen upon him, but the only regret he felt was that the vision had vanished so quickly. Then, as he turned away, he found that not only had he not lost his sight, but that he could now see with a marvellous clearness. He saw the road, and even the foot-prints and grains of sand on the road; the hut, and the reeds on the hut; the moor, and the boulders and the rowan-trees on the moor. Everything was as distinct as if it had been—not daylight, but as if the air were of the clear colour of a nut-brown brook in summer.

Praising God for all His goodness he returned home, and as he went he looked back once and again and yet again, and each time he saw the twelve awful figures in strange cloth-ing, guarding the lonely thatched hovel on the edge of the moor.

After this there were no more stories told of Mary, and no one even dared speak to her of the wonderful manner in which her prayer was answered, so that she never knew what the old Vicar had seen. But late at night people would rather go a great way round than take the road which passed by her poor hut.

William Canton

ON THE SHORES OF LONGING

It was in the old forgotten days when all the western coast of Spain was sprinkled with lonely hermitages among the rocks, and with holy houses and towers of prayer; and this west coast was thought to be the last and outermost edge of all land, for beyond there lay nothing but the vast ocean stream and the sunset. There, in the west of the world, on the brink of the sea and the lights of the day that is done, lived the men of God, looking for ever towards the east for the coming of the Lord. Even the dead were laid in the place of their resurrection with their feet pointing to the morning, so that when they should arise their faces would be turned towards His coming. Thus it came to pass that the keen white wind out of the east was named the wind of the dead men's feet.

Now in one or these holy houses lived the monk Bresal of the Songs, who had followed Sedulius the Bishop into Spain.

Bresal had been sent thither to teach the brethren the music of the choirs of the Isle of the Gael and to train the novices in chant and psalmody, for of all singers the sweetest was he, and he could play on every instrument of wind or string, and was skilled in all the modes of minstrelsy. Thereto he knew by heart numberless hymns and songs and poems, and God had given him the gift to make songs and hymns, and beautiful airs for the singing of them. And for these things, so sweet and gentle was the nature of the man, he was greatly beloved whithersoever he fared.

A happy and holy life had he lived, but now he was growing old; and as he looked from the convent on the cliffs far over the western waters, he thought daily more and more of Erinn, and a great longing grew upon him to see once more that green isle in which he had been born. And when he saw, far below, the ships of the sea-farers dragging slowly away into the north in the breezy sunshine or in the blue twilight, his eyes became dim with the thought that perchance these wind-reddened mariners might be steering for the shores of his longing.

The Prior of the convent noticed his sadness and questioned him of the cause, and when Bresal told him, "Why should you go?" he asked. "Do you not love us any longer?"

"Dearly do I love you, father," replied Bresal, "and dearly this house, and every rock and tree and flower; but no son of the Isle of the Gael forgets the little mother-lap of earth whereon he was nursed, or the smell of the burning peat, or the song of the robin, or the drone of the big mottled wild bee, or the cry of the wild geese when the winter is nigh. Even Columba the holy pined for the lack of these things. This is what he says in one of the songs which he has left us:

There's an eye of grey
Looks back to Erinn far away;
Big tears wet that eye of grey
Seeking Erinn far away."

Now the Prior loved Bresal as Jonathan loved David; and though it grieved him to part with him, he resolved that if it could be compassed Bresal should go back to his own country. "But you must never forget us, and when you are happy, far away from us, you must think of us and give us your heart in prayer."

"Never shall I forget you, father," the Singer replied. "Indeed, it will not be a strange thing if I shall long for you then even as I am longing for my home now; for in truth, next to my home, most do I love the brethren of this house, and the very house itself, and the hills and the sea and the dying lights of the evening. But I know that it will not be permitted me ever to return. The place of my birth will be the place of my resurrection."

The Prior smiled, and laid his hand gently on the monk's shoulder: "O Bresal, if it be within my power you shall have your will."

So he sent messengers to Sedulius the Bishop; and Sedulius, who also had the Irish heart with its tears of longing, consented; and not many days after the swallows and martins had gone flashing by into the north, Bresal of the Songs was free to follow as speedily as he might.

Long was the way and weary the pilgrimage, but at last he reached the beloved green Isle of the Gael, and fared into the south-west—and this is the land in which it is told that Patrick the Saint celebrated Mass on every seventh ridge he passed over. He came at sunset on the last day of the week to the place of bells and cells among the rocks of the coast of Kerry. In that blessed spot there is ever a service of Angels ascending and descending. And when he saw once more the turf dyke and the wattled cells and the rude stone church of the brotherhood where he had been a son of reading in his boyhood, and the land all quiet with the labour of the week done, and the woods red with the last light of the finished day, the tears ran down his face, and he fell on the earth and kissed it for joy at his return. It was a glad thing for him to be there once more; to recognise each spot he had loved, to look on the old stones and trees, the hills and sparkling sea, the rocky isle and the curraghs of the fisher-folk; to smell the reek of the peat curling up blue in the sweet air; for all these things had haunted him in dreams when he was in a distant land.

Now when the first hunger of longing had been appeased, and the year wore round, and the swallows gathered in the autumn, and every bush and tree was crowded with them while they waited restlessly for a moonlight night and a fair wind to take their flight over sea, Bresal began to think tenderly of the home on the Spanish cliffs overhanging the brink of the sunset.

Then in the brown days of the autumn rains; and again in the keen November when the leaves were falling in sudden showers—but the highest leaves clung the longest—and puffs of whirling wind set the fallen leaves flying, and these were full of sharp sounds and pattering voices; and sixes of sparrows went flying with the leaves so that one could not well say which were leaves and which were birds; and yet again through the bitter time when the eaves were hung with icicles and the peaks of the blue slieves were white with snow, and the low hills and fields were hoary—the memory of the Prior and of the beloved house prevailed with him and he felt the dull ache of separation.

As the days passed by his trouble grew the greater, for he began to fear that his love of the creature was attaching him too closely to the earth and to the things of this fleeting life of our exile. In vain he fasted and prayed and strove to subdue his affections; the human heart within him would not suffer him to rest.

Now it happened on a day when the year had turned, and a

William Canton

soft wind was tossing the little new leaves and the shadows of the leaves and the new grass and the shadows of the grass, Bresal was sitting on a rock in the sun on the hillside.

Suddenly there flashed by him, in a long swift joyous swing of flight, two beautiful birds with long wings and forked tails and a sheen of red and green. It was the swallows that had returned.

For a moment he felt an ascension of the heart, and then he recollected that nearly a year had elapsed since he had seen the face of his friend the Prior for the last time in this world. And he wondered to himself how they all fared, whether any one had died, what this one or that was now doing, whether they still spoke at times of him, but chiefly he thought of the Prior, and he prayed for him with a great love. And thinking thus as he sat on the rock, Bresal seemed to see once more the dear house in Spain and the cliffs overlooking the vast ocean stream, and it appeared to him as though he were once again in a favourite nook among the rocks beside the priory.

In that nook a thread of water trickled down into a hollow stone and made a little pool, and around the pool grew an ice-plant with thick round green leaves set close and notched on the edge, and a thin russet stalk, and little stars of white flowers sprinkled with red. And hard by the pool stood a small rounded evergreen tree from which he had often gathered the orange-scarlet berries. At the sight of these simple and familiar things the tears ran down Bresal's cheeks, half for joy and half for sorrow.

Now at this selfsame moment the Prior was taking the air and saying his office near that very spot, and when he had closed his breviary, he remembered his friend in Erinn far away, and murmured, "How is it, Lord, with Bresal my brother? Have him, I pray Thee, ever in Thy holy keeping."

As he spoke the gift of heavenly vision descended on the Prior, and he saw where Bresal sat on a rock in the sun gazing at the evergreen tree and the ice-plant about the little pool, and he perceived that Bresal fancied he was looking at these things.

A great tenderness for Bresal filled the Prior's heart, and he prayed: "Lord, if it be Thy holy will, let Bresal my brother have near him these things of which he is dreaming, as a remembrance of what his soul loveth." Then, turning to the tree and the plant and the pool, he blessed them and said: "O little tree and starry plant and cool well and transparent fern, and whatsoever else Bresal now sees, arise in the name of the Lord of the four winds and of earth and water and fire, arise and go and make real the dream that he is dreaming."

As he spoke the trickling water and the tree and the saxifrage, and with them parcels of soil and rock, and with the pool the blue light of the sky reflected in it, rose like a cloud and vanished, and the Prior beheld them no more.

At last Bresal brushed away his tears, blaming his weakness and his enslavement to earthly affections, but the things he had seen in his happy day-dream did not vanish. To his great amazement, there at his feet were the little pool and the ice-plant, and hard by grew the evergreen tree. He rose with a cry of joy, "O Father Prior, 'tis thy prayer hath done this!"

And care was lifted from him, for now he knew that in his human love he had in nowise sinned against the love of God, but contrariwise the love of his friend had drawn him closer to the love of his Maker. During all the days of the years of his exile this little parcel of Spain was a solace and a strength to him.

Many a hundred years has gone by since this happened, but

William Canton

still if you travel in that land you may see the ice-plant and the evergreen tree. And the name of the evergreen is the Strawberry Tree. The ice-plant, which is also called a saxifrage, may now be seen in many a garden to which it has been brought from the Kerry mountains, and it is known as London Pride. Botanists who do not know the story of Bresal of the Songs have been puzzled to explain how a Spanish tree and a Spanish flower happen to grow in one little nook of Erinn.

THE CHILDREN OF SPINALUNGA

The piazza or square in front of the Cathedral was the only open space in which the children of Spinalunga had room to play. Spinalunga means a Long Spine or Ridge of rock, and the castello or little walled town which bore that name was built on the highest peak of the ridge, inside strong brown stone walls with square towers. So rough and steep was this portion of the ridge that the crowded houses, with their red roofs and white gables, were piled up one behind another, and many of the streets were narrow staircases, climbing up between the houses to the blue sky.

On the top the hill was flat, and there the Cathedral stood, and from her niche above the great west entrance the beautiful statue of the Madonna with the Babe in her arms looked across the square, and over the huddled red roofs, and far away out to the hills and valleys with their evergreen oaks and plantations of grey olives, and bright cornfields and vineyards.

On three sides the town was sheltered by hills, but a very deep ravine separated them from the ridge, so that on those three sides it was impossible for an enemy to attack the town. On the nearest hills great pine woods grew far up the slopes, and sheltered it from the east winds which blew over the snowy peaks.

William Canton

Now on the southern side of the square stood the houses of the Syndic and other wealthy citizens, with open colonnades of carved yellow stone; and all about the piazza at intervals there were orange-trees and pomegranates, growing in huge jars of red earthenware.

This had been the children's playground as long as any one could remember, but in the days of the blessed Frate Agnolo the Syndic was a grim, childless, irascible old man, terribly plagued with gout, which made him so choleric that he could not endure the joyous cries and clatter of the children at their play. So at last in his irritation he gave orders that, if the children must play at all, it would have to be in their own dull narrow alleys paved with hard rock, or outside beyond the walls of the castello. For their part the youngsters would have been glad enough to escape into the green country among the broom and cypress, the red snapdragon and golden asters and blue pimpernels, but these were wild and dangerous times, and at any moment a troop of Free-lances from Pisa or a band of Lucchese raiders might have swept down and carried them off into captivity.

They had therefore to sit about their own doors, and the piazza of the Cathedral became strangely silent in the summer evenings, and there was a feeling of dulness and discontent in the little town. Never a whit better off was the Syndic, for he was now angry with the stillness and the deserted look of the square.

In the midst of this trouble the blessed Brother Agnolo came down from his hermitage among the pine woods, and when he heard of what had taken place, he went straightway to the Syndic and took him to task, with soft and gracious words.

"Messer Gianni, pain I know will often take all sweetness out of the temper of a man, but in this you are not doing well.

There is no child in Spinalunga but would readily forego all his happy play to give you ease and solace, but in this way they cannot help you. By sending them away you do but cloud their innocent lives, and you are yourself none the better for their absence. Were it not wiser for you to seek to distract yourself in their harmless merry-making? I may well think that you have never watched them at their sports; but if you will bid them come back to-day, and will but walk a little way with me, you shall see that which shall give you content and delight so great, that never again will you wish to banish them, but will rather pray to have their companionship at all times."

Now the Frate so prevailed on the Syndic that he gave consent, and bade all the children, lass and lad, babe and prattler, come to the square for their games as they used to do. And leaning with one hand on his staff, and with the other on the shoulder of Brother Agnolo, he moved slowly through the fruit-trees in the great jars to the steps of the Cathedral.

Suddenly the joy-bells began to ring, and the little people came laughing and singing and shouting from the steep streets and staircases and alleys, and they raced and danced into the piazza like Springtime let loose, and they chased each other, and caught hands and played in rings, and swarmed among the jars, as many and noisy as swallows when they gather for their flight over sea in the autumn-tide.

"Look well, Messer Gianni," said the Frate, "and perceive who it is that shares their frolics."

As the Brother spoke the eyes of the Syndic were opened; and there, with each little child, was his Angel, clothed in white, and white-winged; and as the little folk contended together, their Angels contended with each other; and as they ran and danced and sang, so ran and danced and sang their Angels. Which was the laughter of the children, and which that of the Angels, the Syndic could not tell; and when the plump two-year-olds tottered and tumbled, their Angels caught them and saved them from hurt; and even if they did weep and make a great outcry, it was because they were frightened, not because they were injured, and straightway they had forgotten what ailed them and were again merrily trudging about.

In the midst of this wonderful vision of young Angels and bright-eyed children mingling so riotously together, the Syndic heard an inexpressibly joyous laugh behind him. Turning his head, he saw that it was the little marble Babe in the arms of the Madonna. He was clapping his hands, and had thrown back his head against his mother's bosom in sudden delight.

Did the Syndic truly see this? He was certain he did—for a moment; and yet in that same moment he knew that the divine Babe was once more a babe of stone, with its sweet grave face and unconscious eyes; and when the Syndic turned again to watch the children, it was only the children he saw; the Angels were no longer visible.

"It is not always given to our sinful eyes to see them," said Brother Agnolo, answering the Syndic's thought, "but whether we see them or see them not, always they are there."

Now it was in the autumn of the same year that the fierce captain of Free-lances, the Condottiere Ghino, appeared one moonlight night before the gates of Spinalunga, and bade the guard open in the name of Pisa.

As I have said, the little hill-town could only be attacked on the western side, on account of the precipitous ravine which divided it from the hills; but the ridge before the gate was crowded with eight hundred horsemen and two thousand men-at-arms clamouring to be admitted. Nothing daunted, the garrison on the square towers cried back a defiance; the war-bell was sounded; and the townspeople, men and women, hurried down to defend the walls.

After the first flight of arrows and quarrels the Free-lances fell back out of bowshot, and encamped for the night, but the hill-men remained on the watch till daybreak. Early in the morning Ghino himself rode up the ascent with a white flag, and asked for a parley with the Syndic.

"We are from Pisa," said the Condottiere; "Florence is against us; this castello we must hold for our safety. If with your good-will, well and good!"

"We are bound by our loyalty to Florence," replied the Syndic briefly.

"The sword cuts all bonds," said the Free-lance, with a laugh; "but we would gladly avoid strife. Throw in your lot with us. All we ask is a pledge that in the hour of need you will not join Florence against us."

"What pledge do you ask?" inquired the Syndic.

"Let twenty of your children ride back with us to Pisa," said the Free-lance. "These shall answer for your fidelity. They shall be cherished and well cared for during their sojourn."

Who but Messer Gianni was the angry man on hearing this?

"Our children!" he cried; "are we, then, slaves, that we must needs send you our little ones as hostages? Guards, here! Shoot me down this brigand who bids me surrender your children to him!"

Bolts flew whizzing from the cross-bows; the Free-lance shook his iron gauntlet at the Syndic, and galloped down the ridge unharmed. The Syndic forgot his gout in his wrath, and bade the hill-men hold their own till their roofs crumbled about their ears.

Then began a close siege of the castello; but on the fourth day Frate Agnolo passed boldly through the lines of the enemy, and was admitted through the massive stone gateway which was too narrow for the entrance of either cart or waggon. Great was the joy of the hill-men as the Brother appeared among them. He, they knew, would give them wise counsel and stout aid in the moment of danger.

When they told him of the pledge for which the besiegers asked, he only smiled and shook his head. "Be of good cheer," he said, "God and His Angels have us in their keeping."

Thoughtfully he ascended the steep streets to the piazza, and, entering the Cathedral, he remained there for a long while absorbed in prayer. And as he prayed his face brightened with the look of one who hears joyful news, and when he rose from his knees he went to the house of the Syndic, and spoke with him long and seriously.

At sunset that day a man-at-arms went forth from the gates of the castello with a white flag to the beleaguering lines, and demanded to be taken into the presence of the captain. To him he delivered this message from the Syndic: "To-morrow in the morning the gate of Spinalunga will be thrown open, and all the children of our town who are not halt or blind or ailing shall be sent forth. Come and choose the twenty you would have as hostages."

By the camp-fires that night the Free-lances caroused loud and long; but in the little hill-town the children slept sound while the men and women prayed with pale stern faces. An hour after midnight all the garrison from the towers and all the strong young men assembled in the square. They were divided into two bands, and were instructed to descend cautiously by rope-ladders into the ravine on the eastern side of the town. Thence without sound of tongue or foot they were to steal through the darkness till they had reached certain positions on the flanks of the besiegers, where they were to wait for the signal of onset. Frate Agnolo gave each of them his blessing, as one by one they slid over the wall on to the rope-ladders and disappeared in the blackness of the ravine. Noiselessly they marched under the walls of the town till they reached their appointed posts, and there they lay hidden in the woods till morning.

The Free-lances were early astir. As the first ray of golden light streamed over the pine woods on to the ridge and the valley, the bells of the Cathedral began to ring; the heavy gate of the castello was flung open, and the children trooped out laughing and gay, just as they had burst into the square a few months ago, for this, they were told, was to be a great feast and holiday. As they issued through the deep stone archway they filed to right or left, and drew up in long lines across the width of the ridge. Then raising their childish voices in a simple hymn, they all moved together down the rough slope to the lines of the besiegers. Brother Agnolo, holding a plain wooden cross high above his head, led the way, singing joyously.

It was a wonderful sight in the clear shining air of the hills, and hundreds of women weeping silently on the walls crowded together to watch it; and as they watched they held their breath, for suddenly in the golden light of the morning they saw that behind each child there was a great

William Canton

white-winged Angel with a fiery spear.

Then, as that throng of singing children and shining spirits swept down upon the Free-lances, a wild cry of panic arose from the camp. The eight hundred horsemen turned in dismay, and plunged through the ranks of the men-at-arms, and the mercenaries fell back in terror and confusion, striking each other down and trampling the wounded underfoot in their frantic efforts to escape. At that moment the hill-men who were lying in ambush on each flank bore down on the bewildered multitude, and hacked and hewed right and left till the boldest and hardiest of the horsemen broke and fled, leaving their dead and dying on the field.

So the little hill-town of Spinalunga was saved by the children and their Angels, and even to this day the piazza of the Cathedral is their very own playground, in which no one can prevent them from playing all the year round.

THE SIN OF THE PRINCE BISHOP

The Prince Bishop Evrard stood gazing at his marvellous Cathedral; and as he let his eyes wander in delight over the three deep sculptured portals and the double gallery above them, and the great rose window, and the ringers' gallery, and so up to the massive western towers, he felt as though his heart were clapping hands for joy within him. And he thought to himself, "Surely in all the world God has no more beautiful house than this which I have built with such long labour and at so princely an outlay of my treasure." And thus the Prince Bishop fell into the sin of vainglory, and, though he was a holy man, he did not perceive that he had fallen, so filled with gladness was he at the sight of his completed work.

In the double gallery of the west front there were many great statues with crowns and sceptres, but a niche over the central portal was empty, and this the Prince Bishop intended to fill with a statue of himself. It was to be a very small simple statue, as became one who prized lowliness of heart, but as he looked up at the vacant place it gave him pleasure to think that hundreds of years after he was dead people would pause before his effigy and praise him and his work. And this, too, was vainglory.

As the Prince Bishop lay asleep that night a mighty

William Canton

six-winged Angel stood beside him and bade him rise. "Come," he said, "and I will show thee some of those who have worked with thee in building the great church, and whose service in God's eyes has been more worthy than thine." And the Angel led him past the Cathedral and down the steep street of the ancient city, and though it was midday, the people going to and fro did not seem to see them. Beyond the gates they followed the shelving road till they came to green level fields, and there in the middle of the road, between grassy banks covered white with cherry blossom, two great white oxen, yoked to a huge block of stone, stood resting before they began the toilsome ascent.

"Look!" said the Angel; and the Prince Bishop saw a little blue-winged bird which perched on the stout yoke beam fastened to the horns of the oxen, and sang such a heavenly song of rest and contentment that the big shaggy creatures ceased to blow stormily through their nostrils, and drew long tranquil breaths instead.

"Look again!" said the Angel. And from a hut of wattles and clay a little peasant girl came with a bundle of hay in her arms, and gave first one of the oxen and then the other a wisp. Then she stroked their black muzzles, and laid her rosy face against their white cheeks. Then the Prince Bishop saw the rude teamster rise from his rest on the bank and cry to his cattle, and the oxen strained against the beam and the thick ropes tightened, and the huge block of stone was once more set in motion.

And when the Prince Bishop saw that it was these fellow-workers whose service was more worthy in God's eyes than his own, he was abashed and sorrowful for his sin, and the tears of his own weeping awoke him. So he sent for the master of the sculptors and bade him fill the little niche over the middle portal, not with his own effigy but with an image of the child; and he bade him make two colossal figures of the white oxen; and to the great wonderment of the people these were set up high in the tower so that men could see them against the blue sky. "And as for me," he said, "let my body be buried, with my face downward, outside the great church, in front of the middle entrance, that men may trample on my vainglory and that I may serve them as a stepping-stone to the house of God; and the little child shall look on me when I lie in the dust."

Now the little girl in the niche was carved with wisps of hay in her hands, but the child who had fed the oxen knew nothing of this, and as she grew up she forgot her childish service, so that when she had grown to womanhood and chanced to see this statue over the portal she did not know it was her own self in stone. But what she had done was not forgotten in heaven.

And as for the oxen, one of them looked east and one looked west across the wide fruitful country about the foot of the hill-city. And one caught the first grey gleam, and the first rosy flush, and the first golden splendour of the sunrise; and the other was lit with the colour of the sunset long after the lowlands had faded away in the blue mist of the twilight. Weary men and worn women looking up at them felt that a gladness and a glory and a deep peace had fallen on the life of toil. And then, when people began to understand, they said it was well that these mighty labourers, who had helped to build the house, should still find a place of service and honour in the house; and they remembered that the Master of the house had once been a Babe warmed in a manger by the breath of kine. And at the thought of this men grew more pitiful to their cattle, and to the beasts in servitude, and to all dumb animals. And that was one good fruit which sprang from the Prince Bishop's repentance.

William Canton

Now over the colossal stone oxen hung the bells of the Cathedral. On Christmas Eve the ringers, according to the old custom, ascended to their gallery to ring in the birth of the Babe Divine. At the moment of midnight the master ringer gave the word, and the great bells began to swing in joyful sequence. Down below in the crowded church lay the image of the new-born Child on the cold straw, and at His haloed head stood the images of the ox and the ass. Far out across the snow-roofed city, far away over the white glistening country rang the glad music of the tower. People who went to their doors to listen cried in astonishment: "Hark! what strange music is that? It sounds as if the lowing of cattle were mingled with the chimes of the bells." In truth it was so. And in every byre the oxen and the kine answered the strange sweet cadences with their lowing, and the great stone oxen lowed back to their kin of the meadow through the deep notes of the joy-peal.

In the fulness of time the Prince Bishop Evrard died and was buried as he had willed, with his face humbly turned to the earth; and to this day the weather-wasted figure of the little girl looks down on him from her niche, and the slab over his grave serves as a stepping-stone to pious feet.

THE LITTLE BEDESMAN OF CHRIST

This is the legend of Francis, the Little Bedesman of Christ. Seven hundred years ago was he born in Assisi, the quaint Umbrian town among the rocks; and for twenty years and more he cherished but one thought, and one desire, and one hope; and these were that he might lead the beautiful and holy and sorrowful life which our Lord lived on the earth, and that in every way he might resemble our Lord in the purity and loveliness of His humanity.

Home and wealth and honour he surrendered, and the love of a wife and of little prattlers on his knees; for none of these things were the portion of Christ.

No care he took as to how he should be sheltered by night or wherewith he should be clothed by day; and for meat and drink he looked to the hand of God, for these were to be the daily gift of His giving. So that when he heard the words of the sacred Gospel read in the little church of St. Mary of the Angels—"Provide neither gold nor silver nor brass in your purses, nor scrip for your journey, neither two coats, neither shoes, nor yet staves"—he went out and girt his coarse brown dress with a piece of cord, and cast away his shoes and went barefoot thenceforth.

Even to this day the brethren of the great Order of religious

William Canton

men which he founded are thus clothed, and girt with a cord, and shod with nakedness. And this Order is the Order of the Lesser Brethren, the Fratres Minores; and often they are called Franciscans, or the Friars of St. Francis.

But as to the thought he bestowed on his eating and drinking: once when he and Brother Masseo sat down on a broad stone near a fresh fountain to eat the bread which they had begged in the town, St. Francis rejoiced in their prosperity, saying, "Not only are we filled with plenty, but our treasure is of God's own providing; for consider this bread which has come to us like manna, and this noble table of stone fit for the feasting of kings, and this well of bright water which is beverage from heaven;" and he besought God to fill their hearts with an ardent love of the affluence of holy poverty.

Even the quiet and blessed peace of the cloister and the hermitage he denied himself; for he remembered that though the Lord Christ withdrew into the hills and went into the wilderness to refresh His soul with prayer and communion with His Heavenly Father, it was among the sons of men that He had His dwelling all His days. So he, too, the Little Bedesman, often tasted great happiness among the rocks and trees of solitary places; and his spirit felt the spell of the lonely hills; and he loved to pray in the woods, and in their shadow he was consoled by the visits of Angels, and was lifted bodily from the earth in ecstasies of joy. But the work which he had set his hands to do was among men, and in villages and the busy streets of cities.

It was not in the first place to save their own souls and to attain to holiness that he and his companions abandoned the common way of life. Long afterwards, when thousands of men had joined his Order of the Lesser Brethren, he said: "God has gathered us into this holy Order for the salvation of the world, and between us and the world He has made this compact, that we shall give the world a good example, and the world shall make provision for our necessities."

Yet, though he preached repentance and sorrow for sin, never was it his wish that men and women who had other duties should abandon those duties and their calling to follow his example. Besides the Order of the Lesser Brethren, he had founded an Order of holy women who should pray and praise while the men went forth to teach; but well he knew that all could not do as these had done, that the work of the world must be carried on, the fields ploughed and reaped, and the vines dressed, and the nets cast and drawn, and ships manned at sea, and markets filled, and children reared, and aged people nourished, and the dead laid in their graves; and when people were deeply moved by his preaching and would fain have followed him, he would say: "Nay, be in no unwise haste to leave your homes; there, too, you may serve God and be devout and holy;" and, promising them a rule of life, he founded the Third Order, into which, whatever their age or calling, all who desired to be true followers of Christ Jesus might be admitted.

Even among those who gave themselves up wholly to the life spiritual he discouraged excessive austerity, forbidding them to fast excessively or to wear shirts of mail and bands of iron on their flesh, for these not only injured their health and lessened their usefulness, but hindered them in prayer and meditation and delight in the love of God. Once, too, when it was revealed to him that a brother lay sleepless because of his weakness and the pinch of hunger, St. Francis rose, and, taking some bread with him, went to the brother's cell, and begged of him that they might eat that frugal fare together. God gave us these bodies of ours, not that we might torture them unwisely, but that we might use their strength and comeliness in His service.

William Canton

So, with little heed to his own comfort, but full of consideration and gentleness for the weakness of others, he and his companions with him went about, preaching and praising God; cheering and helping the reapers and vintagers in the harvest time, and working with the field-folk in the earlier season; supping and praying with them afterwards; sleeping, when day failed, in barns or church porches or leper-hospitals, or may be in an old Etruscan tomb or in the shelter of a jutting rock, if no better chance befell; till at last they came to be known and beloved in every village and feudal castle and walled town among the hills between Rome and Florence. At first, indeed, they were mocked and derided and rudely treated, but in a little while it was seen that they were no self-seekers crazed with vanity, but messengers of heaven, and pure and great-hearted champions of Christ and His poor.

In those days of luxury and rapacity and of wild passions and ruthless bloodshed, it was strange to see these men stripping themselves of wealth and power—for many of the brethren had been rich and noble—and proclaiming the Gospel of the love and gentleness and purity and poverty of Christ. For not only were the brethren under vow to possess nothing whatever in the world, and not only were they forbidden to touch money on any account, but the Order itself was bound to poverty. It could not own great estates or noble abbeys and convents, but was as much dependent on charity and God's providing as the humblest of its friars.

Was it a wonderful thing that a great affection grew up in the hearts of the people for these preachers of the Cross, and especially for the most sweet and tender of them all, the Little Bedesman of Christ, with the delicate and kindly face worn by fasting, the black eyes, and the soft and sonorous voice? Greatly the common people loved our Lord, and gladly they listened to Him; and of all men who have lived

St. Francis was most like our Lord in the grace and virtue of His humanity. I do not think that ever at any time did he say or do anything till he had first asked himself, What would my Lord have done or said?

And certain it seems to me that he must have thought of the Thief in Paradise and of the divine words Christ spoke to him on the cross, when Brother Angelo, the guardian of a hermitage among the mountains, told him how three notorious robbers had come begging; "but I," said the Brother, "quickly drove them away with harsh and bitter words." "Then sorely hast thou sinned against charity," replied the Saint in a stern voice, "and ill hast thou obeyed the holy Gospel of Christ, who wins back sinners by gentleness, and not by cruel reproofs. Go now, and take with thee this wallet of bread and this little flask of wine which I have begged, and get thee over hill and valley till thou hast found these men; and when thou comest up with them, give them the bread and the wine as my gift to them, and beg pardon on thy knees for thy fault, and tell them that I beseech them no longer to do wrong, but to fear and love God; and if this they will do, I will provide for them so that all their days they shall not lack food and drink." Then Brother Angelo did as he was bidden, and the robbers returned with him and became God's bedesmen and died in His service.

Not to men alone but to all living things on earth and air and water was St. Francis most gracious and loving. They were all his little brothers and sisters, and he forgot them not, still less scorned or slighted them, but spoke to them often and blessed them, and in return they showed him great love and sought to be of his fellowship. He bade his companions keep plots of ground for their little sisters the flowers, and to these lovely and speechless creatures he spoke, with no great fear that they would not understand his words. And all this was a marvellous thing in a cruel time, when human life was

William Canton

accounted of slight worth by fierce barons and ruffling marauders.

For the bees he set honey and wine in the winter, lest they should feel the nip of the cold too keenly; and bread for the birds, that they all, but especially "my brother Lark," should have joy of Christmastide, and at Rieti a brood of redbreasts were the guests of the house and raided the tables while the brethren were at meals; and when a youth gave St. Francis the turtle-doves he had snared, the Saint had nests made for them, and there they laid their eggs and hatched them, and fed from the hands of the brethren.

Out of affection a fisherman once gave him a great tench, but he put it back into the clear water of the lake, bidding it love God; and the fish played about the boat till St. Francis blessed it and bade it go.

"Why dost thou torment my little brothers the Lambs," he asked of a shepherd, "carrying them bound thus and hanging from a staff, so that they cry piteously?" And in exchange for the lambs he gave the shepherd his cloak. And at another time seeing amid a flock of goats one white lamb feeding, he was concerned that he had nothing but his brown robe to offer for it (for it reminded him of our Lord among the Pharisees); but a merchant came up and paid for it and gave it him, and he took it with him to the city and preached about it so that the hearts of those hearing him were melted. Afterwards the lamb was left in the care of a convent of holy women, and to the Saint's great delight, these wove him a gown of the lamb's innocent wool.

Fain would I tell of the coneys that took refuge in the folds of his habit, and of the swifts which flew screaming in their glee while he was preaching; but now it is time to speak of the sermon which he preached to a great multitude of birds in a field by the roadside, when he was on his way to Bevagno. Down from the trees flew the birds to hear him, and they nestled in the grassy bosom of the field, and listened till he had done. And these were the words he spoke to them:

"Little birds, little sisters mine, much are you holden to God your Creator; and at all times and in every place you ought to praise Him. Freedom he has given you to fly everywhere; and raiment He has given you, double and threefold. More than this, He preserved your kind in the Ark, so that your race might not come to an end. Still more do you owe him for the element of air, which he has made your portion. Over and above, you sow not, neither do you reap; but God feeds you, and gives you streams and springs for your thirst; the mountains He gives you, and the valleys for your refuge, and the tall trees wherein to build your nests. And because you cannot sew or spin, God takes thought to clothe you, you and your little ones. It must be, then, that your Creator loves you much, since He has granted you so many benefits. Be on your guard then against the sin of ingratitude, and strive always to give God praise."

And when the Saint ceased speaking, the birds made such signs as they might, by spreading their wings and opening their beaks, to show their love and pleasure; and when he had blessed them with the sign of the cross, they sprang up, and singing songs of unspeakable sweetness, away they streamed in a great cross to the four quarters of heaven.

One more story I must tell of the Saint and the wild creatures.

On a time when St. Francis was dwelling in the town of Agobio, there appeared in that countryside a monstrous grey wolf, which was so savage a man-eater that the people were afraid to go abroad, even when well armed. A pity it was to see folk in such fear and danger; wherefore the Saint, putting his whole trust in God, went out with his companions so far as they dared go, and thence onward all alone to the place where the wolf lay.

The wild beast rushed out at him from his lair with open mouth, but St. Francis waited and made over him the sign of the most holy cross, and called him to him, saying, "Come hither, Brother Wolf! In the name of Christ I bid you do no harm, neither to me nor to any one." And when the wolf closed his jaws and stopped running, and came at the Saint's bidding, as gentle as a lamb, and lay down at his feet, St. Francis rebuked him for the slaying of God's creatures, the beasts, and even men made in God's image. "But fain would I make peace," he said, "between you and these townsfolk; so that if you pledge them your faith that you will do no more scathe either to man or beast, they will forgive you all your offences in the past, and neither men nor dogs shall harry you any more. And I will look to it that you shall always have food as long as you abide with the folk of this countryside."

Whereupon Brother Wolf, by movements of body and tail and bowing of head, gave token of his good will to abide by that bargain. And in sign that he plighted his troth to it he gave the Saint his paw, and followed to the market-place of Agobio, where St. Francis repeated all that he had said, and the people agreed to the bargain, and once more the wolf gave pledge of his faith by putting his paw in the Saint's hand.

For two years thereafter Brother Wolf dwelt in Agobio, going tame and gentle from house to house and in and out at will, doing hurt to none, but much loved of the children and cared for in food and drink and kindness by the townsfolk, so that no one lifted stone or stick against him, neither did any dog bark at him. At the end of those years he died of old age, and the people were grieved that no more should they see his gentle coming and going.

Such was the courtesy and sweet fellowship of St. Francis with the wild creatures.

It remains yet to say of him that he was ever gay and joyous as became God's gleeman. Greatly he loved the song of bird and man, and all melody and minstrelsy. Nor was it ill-pleasing to God that he should rejoice in these good gifts, for once lying in his cell faint with fever, to him came the thought that the sound of music might ease his pain; but when the friar whom he asked to play for him was afraid of causing a scandal by his playing, St. Francis, left alone, heard such music that his suffering ceased and his fever left him. And as he lay listening he was aware that the sound kept coming and going; and how could it have been otherwise? for it was the lute-playing of an Angel, far away, walking in Paradise.

Sweet new songs he made in the language of the common people, folk of field and mountain, muleteers and vine-dressers, woodmen and hunters, so that they in turn might be light of heart amid their toil and sorrow. One great hymn he composed, and of that I will speak later; but indeed all his sayings and sermons were a sort of divine song, and when he sent his companions from one village to another he bade them say: "We are God's gleemen. For song and sermon we ask largesse, and our largesse shall be that you persevere in sorrow for your sins."

Seeing that ladies of the world, great and beautiful, took pleasure in the songs of the troubadours sung at twilight under their windows, he charged all the churches of his Order that at fall of day the bells should be rung to recall the greeting with which Gabriel the Angel saluted the Virgin Mother of the Lord: "Hail, full of grace, the Lord is with thee, blessed art thou among women." And from that day to this the bells have rung out the Angelus at sunset, and now there is no land under heaven wherein those bells are not heard and wherein devout men hearing them do not pause to repeat that greeting angelic.

In like fashion it was great delight to him (the Pope having given him leave) to make in the churches of the Order a representation of the Crib of Bethlehem on the feast of the Nativity. Of these the first was made at the hermitage of Greccio. Thither the peasants flocked on Christmas Eve, with lanterns and torches, making the forest ring with their carols; and there in the church they found a stable with straw, and an ox and an ass tethered to the manger; and St. Francis spoke to the folk about Bethlehem and the Shepherds in the field, and the birth of the divine Babe, so that all who heard him wept happy tears of compassion and thankfulness.

And as St. Francis stood sighing for joy and gazing at the empty manger, behold! a wondrous thing happened. For the knight Giovanni, who had given the ox and the ass and the stable, saw that on the straw in the manger there lay a beautiful child, which awoke from slumber, as it seemed, and stretched out its little hands to St. Francis as he leaned over it.

Even to this day there is no land in which you may not see, on Christmas Eve, the Crib of Bethlehem; but in those old days of St. Francis many souls were saved by the sight of that lowly manger from the sin of those heretics who denied that the Word was made flesh and that the Son of God was born as a little child for our salvation.

The joy and gaiety of St. Francis were of two kinds. There

was the joy of love, and there was the joy of suffering for love. And of this last he spoke a wonderful rhapsody as he journeyed once with Brother Leo, in the grievous cold of the early spring, from Perugia to St. Mary of the Angels. For, as Brother Leo was walking on before, St. Francis called aloud to him:—

"O Brother Leo, although throughout the world the Lesser Brethren were mirrors of holiness and edification, nevertheless write it down, and give good heed to it, that not therein is perfect joy."

And again, a little further on, he called aloud:

"O Brother Leo, though the Lesser Brother should give the blind sight, and make the misshapen straight, and cast out devils, and give hearing to the deaf, and make the lame to walk and the dumb to speak; yea, should he even raise the four days' dead to life, write it down that not herein is perfect joy."

And yet a little further on he cried out:

"O Brother Leo, if the Lesser Brother should know all languages, and every science, and all the Scriptures, so that he could foretell not solely the hidden things of the future but also the secrets of the heart, write down that not therein is perfect joy."

A little further yet, and once again he cried aloud:

"O Brother Leo, God's little sheep, though the Lesser Brother were to speak with the tongue of the Angels, and know the courses of the stars and the virtues of herbs, and though the treasures of the earth were discovered to him, and he had craft and knowledge of birds and fishes and of all living creatures, and of men, and of trees and stones, and roots and waters, write it down that not therein is perfect joy."

And once more, having gone a little further, St. Francis called aloud:

"O Brother Leo, even though the Lesser Brother could by his preaching convert all the unbelievers to the faith of Christ, write down that not therein is perfect joy."

And when, after St. Francis had spoken in this manner for the space of two miles, Brother Leo besought him to reveal wherein might perfect joy be found, St. Francis answered him:

"When we are come, drenched with rain and benumbed with cold and bespattered with mud and aching with hunger, to St. Mary of the Angels, and knock at the door, and the porter asks wrathfully, 'Who are you?' and on our answering, 'Two of your brethren are we,' 'Two gangrel rogues,' says he, 'who go about cheating the world and sorning the alms of the poor; away with you!' and whips the door to, leaving us till nightfall, cold and famished, in the snow and rain; if with patience we bear this injury and harshness and rejection, nowise ruined in our mind and making no murmur of complaint, but considering within ourselves, humbly and in charity, that the porter knows well who we are, and that God sets him up to speak against us—O Brother Leo, write down that therein is perfect joy."

And perfect joy, he added, if, knocking a second time, they brought the porter out upon them, fuming, and bidding them betake themselves to the alms-house, for knaves and thieves, and nevertheless they bore all with patience and with gladness and love. And yet again, he continued, if a third time they knocked and shouted to him, for pity of their hunger and cold and the misery of the night, to let them in, and he came, fierce with rage, crying, "Ah, bold and sturdy vagabonds, now I will pay you," and caught them by the hood, and hurled them into the snow, and belaboured them with a knotty cudgel; and if still, in despite of all pain and contumely, they endured with gladness, thinking of the pains of the blessed Lord Christ, which for love of Him they too should be willing to bear—then might it be truly written down that therein was perfect joy.

This was the perfect joy of the Saint most like to Christ of all the Saints that the world has seen. And of all joys this was the most perfect, seeing that it was by the patient way of tears and tribulation, of bodily pain and anguish of spirit, of humiliation and rejection, that a man might come most nearly to a likeness of Christ.

Through all his gaiety and gladness and benignity he carried in his heart one sorrow, and that was the memory of the Passion of our Lord. Once he was found weeping in the country, and when he was asked whether he was in grievous pain that he wept, "Ah!" he replied, "it is for the Passion of my Lord Jesus that I weep; and for that I should think little shame to go weeping through the whole world."

Two years before his death there befell him that miraculous transfiguration, which, so far as it may be with a sinful son of Adam, made perfect the resemblance between him and the Saviour crucified. And it was after this manner.

In the upper valley of the Arno stream there towers above the pines and giant beeches of the hills a great basalt rock, Alvernia, which looks over Italy, east and west, to the two seas. That rock is accessible by but a single foot-track, and it is gashed and riven by grim chasms, yet withal great oaks and beech-trees flourish atop among the boulders, and there

William Canton

are drifts of fragrant wild flowers, and legions of birds and other wild creatures dwell there; and the lights and colours of heaven play about the rock, and the winds of heaven visit it with wholesome air.

Now a great and wealthy gentleman of Tuscany, Orlando of Chiusi, gave St. Francis that mountain for a hermitage where he could be remote from men, and thither, with three of the brethren most dear to him, the Saint went to spend the forty days of the Fast of St. Michael the Archangel.

Two nights they slept on the way, but on the third day, so worn was St. Francis with fatigue and illness, that his companions were fain to beg a poor peasant to lend them his ass. As they proceeded on their journey the peasant, walking behind the ass, said to St. Francis, "Tell me now, art thou Brother Francis of Assisi?" and when St. Francis said he was, the peasant rejoined, "Look to it, then, that thou strive to be as good as folk take thee to be, so that those who have faith in thee be not disappointed in what they expect to find in thee." And instantly St. Francis got down from the ass, and, kneeling on the ground, kissed the peasant's feet, and thanked him for his brotherly admonition.

So onward they journeyed up the mountain till they came to the foot of Alvernia, and there as St. Francis rested him under an oak, vast flights of birds came fluttering and blithely singing, and alighted on his shoulders and arms, and on his lap, and about his feet. "Not ill-pleased is our Lord, I think," said he, "that we have come to dwell on this mountain, seeing what glee our little brothers and sisters the Birds show at our coming."

Under a fair beech on the top of the rock the brethren built him a cell of branches, and he lived alone in prayer, apart from the others, for the foreknowledge of his death had overshadowed him. Once as he stood by the cell, scanning the shape of the mountain and musing on the clefts and chasms in the huge rocks, it was borne in upon him that the mountain had been thus torn and cloven in the Ninth Hour when our Lord cried with a loud voice, and the rocks were rent. And beside this beech-tree St. Francis was many times uplifted into the air in rapture, and many times Angels came to him, and walked with him for his consolation.

A while later, the brethren laid a tree across a chasm, and St. Francis hid himself in a more lonely place, where no one might hear him when he cried out; and a falcon, which had its nest hard by his cell, woke him for matins, and according as he was more weary or sickly at one time than another, that feathered brother, having compassion on him, woke him later or sooner, and all the long day was at hand to give him companionship.

Here in this wild place, in September, on Holy Cross Day, early in the morning, before the dawn whitened, St. Francis knelt with his face turned to the dark east; and praying long and with great fervour, he besought the Lord Christ Jesus for two graces before he died. And the first was this, that, so far as mortal flesh might bear it, he might feel in his body the torture which our Lord suffered in His Passion; and the second, that he might feel in his heart the exceeding great love for which He was willing to bear such torture.

Now even while he was praying in this wise a mighty six-winged Seraph, burning with light unspeakable, came flying towards him; and St. Francis saw that the Seraph bore within himself the figure of a cross, and thereon the image of a man crucified. Two of the six wings of the Seraph were lifted up over the head of the crucified; and two were spread for flying; and two veiled the whole of the body on the cross.

William Canton

Then as the Seraph drew nigh, the eyes of Christ the crucified looked into the eyes of St. Francis, piercing and sweet and terrible; and St. Francis could scarce endure the rapture and the agony with which that look consumed him, and transfigured him, and burned into his body the similitude of Christ's Passion. For straightway his hands and his feet were pierced through and through with nails; and the heads of the nails were round and black, and the points were bent backward and riveted on the further side of hand and foot; and his right side was opened with the deep thrust of the spear; and the gash was red and blood came dropping from it. Terrible to bear was the ache of those wounds; and for the nails in his feet St. Francis scarce could stand and could not walk at all.

Such was the transfiguration of the Little Bedesman of Christ into His visible semblance on the holy rock Alvernia.

For two years he sustained the ecstasy and anguish of that likeness, but of his sayings and of the wonders he wrought in that time I will not speak.

In those days he composed the Song of the Sun, and often-times sang it, and in many a village and market-place was it sung by the brethren going two by two in their labour for souls. A mighty hymn of praise to the Lord God most high and omnipotent was this Song of the Sun; for in this manner it was that St. Francis sang:

"Praised be Thou, my Lord; by all Thy creatures praised; and chiefly praised by Brother Sun who gives us light of day.

"Through him Thou shinest; fair is he, brilliant with glittering fire; and he through heaven bears, Most High, symbol and sense of thee.

"Praised by Sister Moon be Thou; and praised by all the Stars. These hast Thou made, and Thou hast made them precious and beautiful and bright.

"Praised by Brother Wind be Thou; by Air, and Cloud that lives in air, and all the Weathers of the world, whereby their keep Thou dost provide for all the creatures Thou hast made.

"Praised by Sister Water, Lord, be Thou; the lowly water, precious, pure, the gracious handmaiden.

"Praised by Brother Fire, by whom Thou makest light for us i' the dark; and fair is he and jocund, sturdy and strong.

"Praised by our Sister Mother-Earth, which keeps us and sustains, and gives forth plenteous fruit, and grass, and coloured flowers.

"Praised be Thou, Lord my God, by those who for Thy love forgive, and for Thy love endure; blessed in their patience they; by Thee shall they be crowned."

As he drew nigh to his end at St. Mary of the Angels, he cried out, "Welcome, Sister Death!" and when his brethren, as he had bidden them, sang once more the Song of the Sun, he added another verse:

"Praised by our Sister Death be Thou—that bodily death which no man may escape. Alas for those who die in mortal sin, but happy they conforming to Thy will; for these the second death shall nowise hurt."

In the tenth month, on the fourth day of the month, in the forty-and-fifth year of his age, having recited the Psalm, "I cried unto Thee, O Lord, and said: Thou art my hope and my portion in the land of the living," St. Francis died very joyfully. At the fall of the night he died, and while still the brethren were gazing upon his face there dropped down on the thatch of the cell in which he lay larks innumerable, and most sweetly they sang, as though they rejoiced at the release of their holy kinsman.

He was buried at the great church at Assisi; but though it is thought he lies beneath the high altar, the spot is unknown to any man, and the hill-folk say that St. Francis is not dead at all, but that he lives hidden in a secret crypt far down below the roots of wall and pillar. Standing there, pale and upright, with the blood red in the five wounds of his crucifixion, he waits in a heavenly trance for the sound of the last trumpet, when the nations of the earth shall see in the clouds Him whom they have pierced.

Long after his death it was the custom of the brethren of a certain house of his Order to go chanting in procession at midnight once in the year to his resting-place. But the way was long and dark; the weather often bleak and stormy. Little by little devotion cooled, and the friars fell away, till there remained but one old monk willing to go on this pilgrimage. As he went into the dark and the storm, the road among the woods and rocks grew luminous, and in place of the cross and torches and canticles of the former days, great flocks of birds escorted him on his way, singing and keeping him company. The little feathered brothers and sisters had not abated in their love of the Little Bedesman who had caressed and blessed them.

THE BURNING OF ABBOT SPIRIDION

Many wonderful things are told of the Abbot Spiridion, who lived a hundred years and four and yet grew never old; neither was the brightness of his eyes dimmed nor his hair silvered, nor was his frame bowed and palsied with the weakness of age.

During the long years in which he ruled the abbey he had founded, he seemed to live less in this world than in the communion of the blessed souls of men redeemed. The whole earth was as clear to him as though it had been of crystal, and when he raised his eyes he saw not solely what other men saw, but the vision of all that is under the heavens. And this vision of life was at once his trial and his consolation. For it was an unspeakable sorrow and anguish to see on all sides the sin and suffering and misery of creation, and often he wept bitterly when no one dared ask him the reason of his affliction. Yet oftentimes, on the other hand, he laughed for lightness of spirit, and bade the brethren rejoice because of the salvation of some reprobate soul, or the relief of one oppressed, or the bestowal of some blessing on the servants of God.

When it happened that a brother had been sent on a journey and was long absent, and the community was talking of him, wondering how he had fared and where he might now be, the

William Canton

Abbot would sometimes break silence and say: "I see our brother resting in such or such a cell," or "Our brother is even now singing a psalm as he drifts in his small boat of skins down this or that river," or, perchance, "Our brother is coming over the hill and in an hour he will be with us."

In the abbey there was a certain lay-brother, dull and slow of wit, with a hindrance in his speech; and one of the monks despised him and scoffed at his defect of nature. This lay-brother had the care of the garden of pot-herbs and fruit-trees, and as he was toiling there one day the Abbot called the uncharitable monk to him, and said: "Come, let us see what our brother the Fool is doing."

The monk trembled when he heard those words, for he knew that his scornfulness had been discovered, and he followed the Abbot in great confusion. In the garden they found the lay-brother planting cabbages.

"Is our brother the Fool alone?" asked the Abbot.

"Our brother is alone, father," replied the monk.

Then the Abbot touched the monk's eyes, and straightway he saw that the lay-brother was not alone: beside him were two radiant child-angels, one of whom held for him a basket containing the young plants, and the second walked to and fro playing on a lute to lighten his labour. Then, over-whelmed with shame, the monk fell on his knees, confessing his sin and promising amendment.

More strange than this is the story I have now to tell. It happened through mischance that fire broke out in the abbey, and the flames were spreading so fiercely from one wattled cell to another that there was great danger of the whole monastery being destroyed. With piteous cries the religious surrounded the Abbot, and besought him to intercede with God that their home might be spared.

Spiridion gently shook his head. "The mercy of God," he replied, "has given it to another to intercede for us in our danger this day. The holy Pontiff, Gregory, has looked out of Rome and seen us in our trouble. At this moment he is kneeling in prayer for us, and his supplication on our behalf will avail."

Even while Spiridion was speaking, the Pope, far away in the Golden City, beheld the flames rising from the abbey, and called his household to join him in entreating heaven; and at once it was seen that the flames were being beaten to the ground and extinguished as though invisible hands were beating them down with invisible branches of trees.

Now when the brethren were made aware that the whole earth was being constantly shown thus in vision to the Abbot, they stood in sad dread of him; even the most pure and lowly-hearted were abashed at this thought that perchance every act and every vain fancy of theirs was laid bare to his knowledge. So it came to pass that out of shame and fear their hearts were little by little estranged from him.

The Abbot was not slow to perceive the change, and he spoke of it when they met in chapter.

"Truly it is a grievous and a terrible thing," he said, "that any man should see with the eyes of the soul more than it is given the eye of flesh to see; and I pray you, brethren, beseech the Lord, if it be His will, that the vision be withdrawn from me. But if His will it be not, beseech Him that I may not sin through seeing. So much for myself, but as for you, dear children, why are you grieved? Because it may be that I see you when you think no man sees you? Am I

William Canton

then the only one who sees you? Is there not at least one other—even the high God, from whom the hidden man of the heart is nowise hidden? If you fear His holy eyes, little need you fear the eyes of any sinful man."

Such a one was the Abbot Spiridion. His spirit passed from among men in the hundred and fifth year of his exile, in the third month of the year, on the morning of the resurrection of the Lord Christ, between the white and the red of the morning, when the brethren were singing prime. As he listened to them singing, his cheeks suddenly became flushed with bright colour, and those who were about him, thinking he was in pain, asked if in any way they might relieve him; but he replied in a low voice, "When the heart is glad the face flowers." In a little after that he laughed softly to himself, and so they knew that his end was gladness.

When he died there were three hundred religious in that monastery, and in his stead Samson was made Abbot of Gracedieu.

The body of Spiridion was laid in a stone coffin hard by the abbey church, and to those who had known the holy man it seemed nothing strange that the sick and afflicted should come and kneel by his grave, in the hope that by his inter-cession they might obtain succour in their misery. Certain it is that the blind were restored to sight, and the sick to health, and the painful to great ease; and the fame of these miracles was noised abroad in the world till thousands came in pilgrimage to the spot, and costly gifts—gold and silver and jewels, sheep and cattle, wine and corn, and even charters of large demesnes, fruitful fields and woods and waters—were bestowed as thank-offerings to the saintly man.

Then over his tomb rose a vast and beautiful minster, and the tomb itself was covered with a shrine, brilliant with blue and vermilion and gold and sculptured flowers, and guarded by angels with outspreading wings.

At the beginning Abbot Samson was well pleased, for the great church rose like a dream of heaven, but when he perceived that the constant concourse of people was destroying the hushed contemplation and piety of the house, and that the brethren were distracted with eagerness for gain and luxury and the pride of life, he resolved to make an end. Wherefore after High Mass on the Feast of All Saints he bade the religious walk in procession to the splendid shrine, and there the Abbot, with the shepherd's staff of rule in his hand, struck thrice on the stone coffin, and three times he called aloud: "Spiridion! Spiridion! Spiridion!" and begged him, as he had been founder and first father of that monastery, to listen to the grievance which had befallen them in consequence of the miracles he had wrought from his grave.

And after an indignant recital of their loss of humility, of their lukewarmness, of their desire for excitement and the pageants of the world, of their lust for buildings of stone and pillared walks and plentiful living, he concluded: "Make, then, we beseech thee, no sign from thy sepulchre. Let life and death, and joy and sorrow, and blindness and disease, and all the vicissitudes of this world follow their natural courses. Do not thou, out of compassion for thy fellow-man, interpose in the lawful succession of things. This is what we ask of thee, expecting it of thy love. But if it be that thou deny us, solemnly we declare unto thee, by the obedience which once we owed thee, we shall unearth thy bones and cast them forth from amongst us."

Now whether it was that for some high purpose God delayed the answer to that prayer, or whether it was the folly and superstition of men which gave to things natural the likeness of the miraculous, and even peradventure the folk lied out of a mistaken zeal for the glory of the saints, there was no abatement of the wonders wrought at Spiridion's tomb; and when the Abbot would have forbidden access to the vast crowds of pilgrims, the people resisted with angry violence and threatened fire and bloodshed.

So Samson summoned the wisest and holiest of the brotherhood, and took them into counsel.

"This thing," said he, "cannot be of God, that one of His saints, the founder of this house, should lead into sloth and luxury the children of the house he has founded. Sooner could I believe that this is a malignant snare of the most Evil One, who heals the bodily ailments of a few that he may wreck the immortal souls of many."

Then arose Dom Walaric, the most aged of the monks, and said: "Already, Father Abbot, hast thou spoken judgment. Grievously shall I lament what must be done; but in one way only can we root out this corruption. Let the bones of the holy man be unearthed and cast forth. He in the high heavens will know that we do not use him despitefully, but that of two evils this, indeed, is scarcely to be spoken of as an evil."

Wherefore, in a grassy bay of the land by the river a great pile of faggots was reared, dry and quick for the touch of flame. And the Abbot broke down the shrine and opened the tomb.

When the stone lid of the coffin had been lifted, the religious saw that, though it had been long buried, the body showed no sign of decay. Fresh and uncorrupted it lay in the sacred vestments; youthful and comely of face, despite a marvellous old age and years of sepulture.

With many tears they raised what seemed rather a sleeping

man than a dead, and bore him to the river; and when they had heaped the faggots about him, the Abbot blessed the body and the fuel, and with his own hand set fire to the funeral pile.

The brethren restrained not their weeping and lamentation as they witnessed that hallowed burning; and the Abbot, with heavy eyes, tarried till the last ember had died out. Then were all the ashes of the fire swept together and cast into the fleeting river, which bore them through lands remote into the utmost sea that hath no outland limit save the blue sky and the low light of the shifting stars.

THE COUNTESS ITHA

In the days of King Coeur-de-Lion the good Count Hartmann ruled in Kirchberg in the happy Swabian land. And never had that fair land been happier than it was in those days, for the Count was a devout Christian, a lover of peace in the midst of warlike and rapacious barons, and a ruler just and merciful to his vassals. Among the green and pleasant hills on his domain he had founded a monastery for the monks of St. Benedict, and thither he often rode with his daughter Itha, the delight of his heart and the light of the grim old castle of the Kirchberg; so that, seeing the piety of her father, she grew up in the love and fear of God, and from her gentle mother she learned to feel a deep compassion for the poor and afflicted.

No sweeter maid than she, with her blue eyes and light brown hair, was there in all that land of sturdy men and nut-brown maidens. The people loved the very earth she stood on. In their days of trouble and sorrow she was their morning and their evening star, and they never wearied of praising her goodness and her beauty.

When Itha was in the bloom of her girlhood it befell that the young Count Heinrich of the Toggenburg, journeying home-ward from the famous tournament at Cologne, heard of this peerless flower of Swabia, and turned aside to the Castle of

Kirchberg to see if perchance he might win a good and lovely wife. He was made welcome, and no sooner had he looked on Itha's fair and loving face, and marked with what modesty and courtesy she bore herself, than he heard joy-bells ringing in his heart, and said, "Now, by the blessed cross, here is the pearl of price for me!" Promptly he wooed her with tender words, and with eyes that spoke more than tongue could find words for, and passionate observance, and all that renders a man pleasing to a maid.

And Itha was not loth to be won, for the Count was young and handsome, tall and strong, and famous for feats of arms, and a mighty lord—master of the rich straths and valleys of the Thur River, and of many a burgh and district in the mountains beyond; and yet, despite all this, he, so noble and beautiful, loved her, even her, the little Swabian maid who had never deemed herself likely to come to such honour and happiness. Nor were the kindly father and mother ill-pleased that so goodly a man and so mighty a lord should have their dear child.

So in a little while the Count put on Itha's hand the ring of betrothal, and Itha, smiling and blushing, raised it to her lips and kissed it. "Blissful ring!" said the Count jestingly; "and yet, dearest heart, you do well to cherish it, for it is an enchanted ring, an old ring of which there are many strange stories." Even while he was speaking Itha's heart misgave her, and she was aware of a feeling of doubt and foreboding; but she looked at the ring and saw how massive was the gold and how curiously wrought and set with rare gems, and its brilliancy and beauty beguiled her of her foreboding, and she asked no questions of the stories told of it or of the nature of its enchantment.

Quickly on the betrothal followed the marriage and the leave-taking. With tears in her eyes Itha rode away with her

William Canton

lord, looking back often to the old castle and gazing farewell on the pleasant land and the fields and villages she should not see again for, it might be, many long years. But by her side rode the Count, ever gay and tender, and he comforted her in her sadness, and lightened the way with loving converse, till she put from her all her regret and longing, and made herself happy in their love.

So they journeyed through the rocks and wildwood of the Schwartzwald, and came in view of the blue waters of the lake of Constance glittering in the sun, and saw the vast mountain region beyond with its pine forests, and above the forests the long blue mists on the high pastures, and far over all, hanging like silvery summer clouds in the blue heavens, the shining peaks of the snowy Alps. And here, at last, they were winding down the fruitful valley of the Thur, and yonder, perched on a rugged bluff, rose the stern walls of Castle Toggenburg, with banners flying from the turrets, and the rocky roadway strewn with flowers, and vassals and retainers crowding to welcome home the bride.

Now, for all his tenderness and gaiety and sweetness in wooing, the Count Heinrich was a hasty and fiery man, quickly stirred to anger and blind rage, and in his storms of passion he was violent and cruel. Not long after their home-coming—woe worth the while!—he flashed out ever and anon in his hot blood at little things which ruffled his temper, and spoke harsh words which his gentle wife found hard to bear, and which in his better moments he sincerely repented. Very willingly she forgave him, but though at first he would kiss and caress her, afterwards her very forgiveness and her meekness chafed and galled his proud spirit, so that the first magical freshness of love faded from their life, even as the dew dries on the flower in the heat of the morning.

Not far from the castle, in a clearing in the woods, nestled the little convent and chapel of Our Lady in the Meadow, and thither, attended by one of her pages, the Countess Itha went daily to pray for her husband, that he might conquer the violence of his wild heart, and for herself, that she might not grow to fear him more than she loved him. In these days of her trial, and in the worse days to come, a great consolation it was to her to kneel in the silent chapel and pour out her unhappiness to her whose heart had been pierced by seven swords of sorrow.

Time went by, and when no little angel came from the knees of God to lighten her burden and to restrain with its small hands the headlong passion of her husband, the Count was filled with bitterness of spirit as he looked forward to a childless old age, and reflected that all the fruitful straths of the Toggenburg, and the valleys and townships, would pass away to some kinsman, and no son of his would there be to prolong the memory of his name and greatness. When this gloomy dread had taken possession of him, he would turn savagely on the Countess in his fits of fury, and cry aloud: "Out of my sight! For all thy meekness and thy praying and thy almsgiving, God knows it was an ill day when I set eyes on that fair face of thine!" Yet this was in no way his true thought, for in spite of his lower nature the Count loved her, but it is ever the curse of anger in a man that it shall wreak itself most despitefully on his nearest and best. And Itha, who had learned this in the school of long-suffering, answered never a word, but only prayed the more constantly and imploringly.

In the train of the Countess there were two pages, Dominic, an Italian, whom she misliked for his vanity and boldness, and Cuno, a comely Swabian lad, who had followed her from her father's house. Most frequently when she went to Our Lady in the Meadow she dismissed Dominic and bade Cuno attend her, for in her distress it was some crumb of comfort to see the face of a fellow-countryman, and to speak to him of Kirchberg and the dear land she had left. But Dominic, seeing that the Swabian was preferred, hated Cuno, and bore the lady scant goodwill, and in a little set his brain to some device by which he might vent his malice on both. This was no difficult task, for the Count was as prone to jealousy as he was quick to wrath, and with crafty hint and wily jest and seemingly aimless chatter the Italian sowed the seeds of suspicion and watchfulness in his master's mind.

Consider, then, if these were not days of heartbreak for this lady, still so young and so beautiful, so unlovingly entreated, and so far away from the home of her happy childhood. Yet she bore all patiently and without complaint or murmur, only at times when she looked from terrace or tower her gaze travelled beyond the deep pine-woods, and in a wistful day-dream she retraced, beyond the great lake and the Black Forest, all the long way she had ridden so joyfully with her dear husband by her side.

One day in the springtime, when the birds of passage had flown northward, carrying her tears and kisses with them, she bethought her of the rich apparel in which she had been wed, and took it from the carved oaken coffer to sweeten in the sun. Among her jewels she came upon her betrothal ring, and the glitter of it reminded her of what her lord had said of its enchantment and the strange stories told of it. "Are any of them so sad and strange as mine?" she wondered with tears in her eyes; then kissing the ring in memory of that first kiss she had given it, she laid it on a table in the window-bay, and busied herself with the bridal finery; and while she was so busied she was called away to some cares of her household, and left the chamber.

When she returned to put away her marriage treasures, the betrothal ring was missing. On the instant a cold fear came over her. In vain she searched the coffer and the chamber; in vain she endeavoured to persuade herself that she must have mislaid the jewel, or that perchance the Count had seen it, and partly in jest and partly in rebuke of her carelessness, had taken it. The ring had vanished, and in spite of herself she felt that its disappearance portended some terrible evil. Too fearful to arouse her husband's anger, she breathed no word of her loss, and trusted to time or oblivion for a remedy.

No great while after this, as the Swabian page was rambling in the wood near the convent, he heard a great outcry of ravens around a nest in an ancient fir-tree, and prompted partly by curiosity to know the cause of the disquiet, and partly by the wish to have a young raven for sport in the winter evenings, he climbed up to the nest. Looking into the great matted pack of twigs, heather and lamb's wool, he caught sight of a gold ring curiously chased and set with sparkling gems; and slipping it gleefully on his finger he descended the tree and went his way homeward to the castle.

A few days later when the Count by chance cast his eye on the jewel, he recognised it at a glance for the enchanted ring of many strange stories. The crafty lies of the Italian Dominic flashed upon him; and, never questioning that the Countess had given the ring to her favourite, he sprang upon Cuno as though he would strangle him. Then in a moment he flung him aside, and in a voice of thunder cried for the wildest steed in his stables to be brought forth. Paralysed with fright, the luckless page was seized and bound by the heels to the tail of the half-tame creature, which was led out beyond the drawbridge, and pricked with daggers till it flung off the men-at-arms and dashed screaming down the rocky ascent into the wildwood.

Stung to madness by his jealousy, the Count rushed to the

apartment of the Countess. "False and faithless, false and faithless!" he cried in hoarse rage, and clutching her in his iron grasp, lifted her in the air and hurled her through the casement into the horrible abyss below.

As she fell Itha commended her soul to God. The world seemed to reel and swim around her; she felt as if that long lapse through space would never have an end, and then it appeared to her as though she were peacefully musing in her chair, and she saw the castle of Kirchberg and the pleasant fields lying serene in the sunlight, and the happy villages, each with its great crucifix beside its rustic church, and men and women at labour in the fields. How long that vision lasted she could not tell. Then as in her fall she was passing through the tops of the trees which climbed up the lower ledges of the castle rocks, green leafy hands caught her dress and held her a little, and strong arms closed about her, and yielded slowly till she touched the ground; and she knew that the touch of these was not the mere touch of senseless things, but a contact of sweetness and power which thrilled through her whole being.

Falling on her knees, she thanked God for her escape, and rising again she went into the forest, wondering whither she should betake herself and what she should do; for now she had no husband and no home. She left the beaten track, and plunging through the bracken, walked on till she was tired. Then she sat down on a boulder. Among the pines it was already dusk, and the air seemed filled with a grey mist, but this was caused by the innumerable dry wiry twigs which fringed the lower branches of the trees with webs of fine cordage; and when a ray of the setting sun struck through the pine trunks, it lit up the bracken with emerald and brightened the ruddy scales of the pine bark to red gold. Here it was dry and sheltered, with the thick carpet of pine-needles underfoot and the thick roof of branches overhead: and but for dread of wild creatures she thought she might well pass the night in this place. To-morrow she would wander further and learn how life might be sustained in the forest.

The last ray of sunshine died away; the deep woods began to blacken; a cool air sighed in the high tops of the trees. It was very homeless and lonely. She took heart, however, remembering God's goodness to her, and placing her confidence in His care.

Suddenly she perceived a glimmering of lights among the pines. Torches they seemed, a long way off; and she thought it must be the retainers of the Count, who, finding she had not been killed by her fall, had sent them out to seek for her. The lights drew nearer, and she sat very still, resigned to her fate whatsoever it might be. And yet nearer they came, till at length by their shining she saw a great stag with lordly antlers, and on the tines of the antlers glittered tongues of flame.

Slowly the beautiful creature came up to her and regarded her with his large soft brown eyes. Then he moved away a little and looked back, as though he were bidding her follow him. She rose and walked by his side, and he led her far through the forest, till they came to an overhanging rock beside a brook, and there he stopped.

In this hidden nook of the mountain-forest she made her home. With branches and stones and turf she walled in the open hollow of the rock. In marshy places she gathered the thick spongy mosses, yellow and red, and dried them in the sun for warmth at night in the cold weather. She lived on roots and berries, acorns and nuts and wild fruit, and these in their time of plenty she stored against the winter. Birds' eggs she found in the spring; in due season the hinds, with their young, came to her and gave her milk for many days; the wild bees provided her with honey. With slow and painful toil she wove the cotton-grass and the fibres of the bark of the birch, so that she should not lack for clothing.

In the warm summer months there was a great tranquillity and hushed joy in this hard life. A tender magic breathed in the colour and music of the forest, in its long pauses of windless day-dreaming, in its breezy frolic with the sunshine. The trees and boulders were kindly; and the turf reminded her of her mother's bosom. About her refuge the wild flowers grew in plenty—primrose and blue gentian, yellow cinquefoil and pink geranium, and forget-me-nots, and many more, and these looked up at her with the happy faces of little children who were innocent and knew no care; and over whole acres lay the bloom of the ling, and nothing more lovely grows on earthly hills. Through breaks in the woodland she saw afar the Alpine heights, and the bright visionary peaks of snow floating in the blue air like glimpses of heaven.

But it was a bitter life in the winter-tide, when the forest fretted and moaned, and snow drifted about the shelter, and the rocks were jagged with icicles, and the stones of the brook were glazed with cold, and the dark came soon and lasted long. She had no fire, but, by God's good providence, in this cruel season the great stag came to her at dusk, and couched in the hollow of the rock beside her, and the lights on his antlers lit up the poor house, and the glow of his body and his pleasant breath gave her warmth.

Here, then, dead to the world, dead to all she loved most dearly, Itha consecrated herself body and soul to God for the rest of her earthly years. If she suffered as the wild children of nature suffer, she was free at least from the cares and sorrows with which men embitter each other's existence. Here she would willingly live so long as God willed; here she would gladly surrender her soul when He was pleased to call it home.

The days of her exile were many. For seventeen years she dwelt thus in her hermitage in the forest, alone and forgotten.

Forgotten, did I say? Not wholly. The Count never forgot her. Stung by remorse (for in his heart of hearts he could not but believe her true and innocent), haunted by the recollection of the happiness he had flung from him, wifeless, childless, friendless, he could find no rest or forgetfulness except in the excitement and peril of the battle-field. But the slaughter of men and the glory of victory were as dust and ashes in his mouth. He had lost the joy of life, the pride of race, the exultation of power. For one look from those sweet eyes, over which, doubtless, the hands of some grateful peasant had laid the earth, he would have joyfully exchanged renown and lordship, and even life itself.

At length in the fulness of God's good time, it chanced that the Count was hunting in a distant part of the forest, when he started from its covert a splendid stag. Away through the open the beautiful creature seemed to float before him, and Heinrich followed in hot chase. Across grassy clearings and through dim vistas of pines, over brooks and among boulders and through close underwood, the fleet quarry led him without stop or stay, till at last it reached the hanging rock which was Itha's cell, and there it stood at bay; and alarmed by the clatter of hoofs, a tall pale woman, rudely clad in her poor forest garb, came to the entrance.

Surprised at so strange a sight, the Count drew rein and stared at the woman. Despite the lapse of time and her pallor and emaciation, in an instant he recognised the wife whom he believed dead, and she too recognised the husband she had loved.

William Canton

How shall I tell of all that was said between those two by that lonely hermitage in the depth of the forest? As in the old days, she was eager to forgive everything; but it was in vain that the Count besought her to return to the life which she had forgotten for so many years. Long had she been dead and buried, so far as earthly things were concerned. She would prefer, despite the hardness and the pain, to spend in this peaceful spot what time was yet allotted to her, but that she longed once more to hear the music of the holy bells, to kneel once more before the altar of God.

What plea could Heinrich use to shake her resolution? His shame and remorse, even his love, held him tongue-tied. He saw that she was no longer the meek gentle Swabian maiden who had shrunk and wept at every hasty word and sharp glance of his. He had slain all human love in her; nothing survived save that large charity of the Saints which binds them to all suffering souls on the earth.

Wofully he consented to her one wish. A simple cell was prepared for her in the wood beside the chapel of Our Lady in the Meadow, and there she dwelt until, in a little while, her gentle spirit was called home.

THE STORY OF THE LOST BROTHER

This is the story written in the chronicle of the Priory of Kilgrimol, which is in Amounderness. It tells of the ancient years before that great inroad of the sea which broke down the high firs of the western forest of Amounderness, and left behind it those tracts of sand and shingle that are now called the Blowing Sands. In those days Oswald the Gentle was Prior of Kilgrimol, and he beheld the inroad of the sea; and afterwards he lived through the suffering and sorrow of the great plague of which people now speak as the Black Death.

Of all monks and men he was the sweetest and gentlest, and long before he was chosen Prior, when he had charge of the youths who wished to be monks, he never wearied of teaching them to feel and care for all God's creatures, from the greatest to the least, and to love all God's works, and to take a great joy even in stones and rocks, and water and earth, and the clouds and the blue air. "For," said he, "according to the flesh all these are in some degree our kinsfolk, and like us they come from the hands of God. Does not Mother Church teach us this, speaking in her prayers of God's creature of fire, and His creature of salt, and His creature of flowers?"

When some of the brotherhood would smile at his gentle sayings, he would answer: "Are these things, then, so strange

William Canton

and childish? Rather, was not this the way of the Lord Jesus? You have read how He was in the wilderness forty days, tempted of Satan, and how He was with the wild beasts? All that those words may mean we have not been taught; but well I believe that the wild things came to Him, even as very little children will run to a good man without any doubt of his goodness; and that they recognised His pitifulness and His power to help them; and that He read in their dumb pleading eyes the pain and the travail under which the whole creation groaneth; and that He blessed them, and gave them solace, and told them in some mysterious way of the day of sacrifice and redemption which was drawing near."

Once when the brethren spoke of clearing out the nests from the church tower, because of the clamour of the daws in the morning and evening twilight, the Novice-master—for this was Oswald's title—besought them to remember the words of the Psalmist, King David: "The sparrow hath found an house and the swallow a nest for herself, where she may lay her young, even thine altars, O Lord of Hosts."

As for the novices, many a legend he told them of the Saints and holy hermits who had loved the wild creatures, and had made them companions or had been served by them in the lonely places of the hills and wildwood. And in this, he taught them, there was nothing strange, for in the book of Hosea, it was written that God would make, for those who served Him, a treaty of peace and a league of love with the beasts and the birds of heaven and the creeping things of the earth, and in the book of Job it was said that even the stones of the field should be in friendship with them.

"And this we see," he would say, "in the life of the blessed Bishop Kieran of Saighir, who was the first Saint born in green Erinn. For he wandered away through the land seeking the little well where he was to found his monastery. That well was in the depths of a hoary wood, and when he drew near it the holy bell which he carried rang clear and bright, as it had been foretold him. So he sat down to rest under a tree, when suddenly a wild boar rushed out of its lair against him; but the breath of God tamed it, and the savage creature became his first disciple, and helped him to fell small trees and to cut reeds and willows so that he might build him a cell. After that there came from brake and copse and dingle and earth and burrow all manner of wild creatures; and a fox, a badger, a wolf, and a doe were among Kieran's first brotherhood. We read, too, that for all his vows the fox made but a crafty and gluttonous monk, and stole the Saint's leather shoes, and fled with them to his old earth. Wherefore Kieran called the religious together with his bell, and sent the badger to bring back the fugitive, and when this was done the Saint rebuked the fox for an unworthy and sinful monk, and laid penance upon him."

When the novices laughed at this adventure, Father Oswald said:

"These things are not matters of faith; you may believe them or not as you will. Perhaps they did not happen in the way in which they are now told, but if they are not altogether true, they are at least images and symbols of truth. But this I have no doubt is true—that when the blessed Columba was Abbot in Iona, he called one of the brethren to him and bade him go on the third day to the western side of the island, and sit on the sea-shore, and watch for a guest who would arrive, weary and hungry, in the afternoon. And the guest would be a crane, beaten by the stormy winds, and it would fall on the beach, unable to fly further. 'And do thou,' said Columba, 'take it up with gentle hands and carry it to the house of the guests, and tend it for three days and three nights, and when it is refreshed it will fly up into the air, and after scanning its path through the clouds it will return to its old sweet home in

Erinn; and if I charge thee so earnestly with this service, it is because the guest comes from our dear land.' And the Brother obeyed; and on the third day the crane arrived, storm-beaten and weary, and three days later it departed. Have you not also heard or read how our own St. Godrich at Whitby protected the four-footed foresters, and how a great stag, which had been saved by him from the hunters, came year after year at a certain season to visit him?"

Many legends too he told them of birds as well as beasts, and three of these I will mention here because they are very pleasant to listen to. One was of St. Malo and the wren. The wren, the smallest of all birds, laid an egg in the hood which St. Malo had hung up on a branch while he was working in the field, and the blessed man was so gentle and loving that he would not disturb the bird, but left his hood hanging on the tree till the wren's brood was hatched.

Then there was the legend of St. Meinrad, who lived in a hut made of boughs on Mount Etzel, and had two ravens for his companions. Now it happened that two robbers wandered near the hermitage, and foolishly thinking that some treasure might be hidden there, they slew the Saint. After a long search, in which they found nothing, they went down the mountain to Zurich; but the holy man's ravens followed them with fierce cries, whirling about their heads and dashing at their faces, so that the people in the valley wondered at the sight. But one of the dalesmen who knew the ravens sent his son to the hermitage to see if all was well, and followed the fellows to the town. There they took refuge in a tavern, but the ravens flew round and round the house, screaming and pecking at the window near which the robbers had seated themselves. Speedily the lad came down with the news of the cruel murder; the robbers were seized, and, having confessed their crime, they suffered the torture of death on the wheel.

And lastly there was the legend of St. Servan, who had a robin which perched on his shoulder, and fed from his hand, and joined in with joyful twittering when the Saint sang his hymns and psalms. Now the lads in the abbey-school were jealous of the Saint's favourite pupil, Kentigern, and out of malice they killed the robin and threw the blame on Kentigern. Bitterly the innocent child wept and prayed over the dead bird; and behold! when the Saint came from singing nones in the minster, the robin fluttered up and flew away to meet him, chirruping merrily.

"A thoughtless thing of little blame," said the Novice-master, "was the wickedness of these boys compared with that of the monks of the Abbot Eutychus. The Abbot had a bear to tend his sheep while he was absent and to shut them in their fold at sunset, and when the monks saw that marvel, instead of praising God they were burned up with envy and ill-will, and they killed the bear. Ah, children, it is still possible for us, even in these days, to kill a Saint's robin and an abbot's bear. Let us beware of envy and jealousy and uncharitableness."

In those years when Father Oswald was thus teaching his novices gentleness and compassion, he had but one trouble in his life, and that was the remembrance of a companion of his youth, who had fled from the Priory and disappeared in the noise and tumult of the world's life. As scholars they had been class-mates, and as novices they had been so closely drawn together that each had pledged to the other that whoever died first should, under God's permission, appear to the one still left alive, and reveal to his friend all that may be told of the state of the departed. Now hardly had they been professed monks more than a year when this brother broke his vows and deserted his habit, and fled away under cloud of night. Oswald had never forgotten his friend, and had never ceased to grieve and pray for him. It was the great hope and desire of his heart that, having at last proved the vanity of all that the world can give, this Lost Brother would one day return, like the Prodigal Son, to the house of his boyhood.

As the years went by Prior Anselm grew old and sickened, and at length what was mortal of him fell as the leaf that falls and is trodden in the clay; and the Novice-master was elected Prior in his stead.

Now one of the first great works which the new Prior set his hand to was the making of two large fish-ponds for the monastery. "And so," said he, "not only shall we have other than sea-fish for our table, but in case of fire we shall have store of water at hand. Then, too, it is a pleasant thing to look on sweet water among trees, and to watch the many sorts of silvery fish playing in their clear and silent world. And well it becomes our state of life that we should have this, for of our Lord's Disciples many were fishermen, and fish and bread were the last earthly food our dear Master ate. Now of these ponds let the larger be our Lake of Gennesaret, and surely it shall some time happen to us that we shall see the Lord when the bright morning has come, and that our hearts shall be as a fire of coals upon the shore."

Of the earth dug out of the fish pools he piled up a high mound or barrow, and stocked it well with saplings of oak and beech, ash and pine, and flowering bushes; and about the mound a spiral way wound to the top, and from the top one saw to the four winds over the high woods of Amounderness, and on the west, beyond the forest, the white sands of the shore and the fresh sea. When the saplings grew tall and stout, the green leaves shut out all sight of the Priory; even the tower of the church; and above the trees in the bright air it was as though one had got half-way to heaven.

Now after a little while the Prior reared on the high summit a vast cross of oak, rooted firmly amid huge boulders, and the face of our Lord crucified was turned to the west, and His arms were opened wide to the sea and to the passing ships. And beneath the flying sails, far away, the mariners and fisher-folk could see the cross in the sky, and they bared their heads to the calvary of Kilgrimol. So the name of our house and our Christ was known in strange waters and in distant havens.

All that climbing greenwood of the mound was alive with wild creatures, winged and four-footed, and no one was suffered to disquiet or annoy them. To us it seemed that the Prior was as well known to all the wild things far and near as he was to us, for the little birds fluttered about him, and the squirrels leaped from tree to tree along the way he went, and the fawns ran from the covert to thrust their noses into his hand. And in the winter time, if the snow lay deep and there was any dearth, food was made ready for them and they came in flocks and troops to the Priory, knowing well, one would think, that the Prior would be their loving almoner.

Bee-hives, too, he set up, and grew all manner of flowers, both for the use of the little brown toilers and for the joyance of the brethren; and of the flowers he spoke deep and beautiful parables too many to be told of in this book.

Now in the third year of his rule the Prior heard tidings of the companion he had never forgotten, and he took into his confidence one of the religious named Bede, in whom he had great trust, and he told him the story of their friendship. "And now, Bede," he said, "I would have thee go on a long journey, even to the golden city of London, and seek out my friend. He will easily be found, for men know his name, and he hath grown to some repute, and the good things of this world have not been denied him. And in this I rejoice, for when he hath won all his heart may desire, he will the sooner

William Canton

discover how little is the joy and how fleeting the content. And tell him that so long as I am Prior of this house, so long shall this house be a home waiting for his home-coming. Bid him come to me—if but for a little while, then for a little while be it; but if he longs for rest, this shall be the place of his rest until the end. And if these things cannot be now, then let them be when they may be."

And Bede went on his long wayfaring and found the Lost Brother, a man happy and of fair fame, and blessed with wife and child. And the monk sat with the little maid on his knee, and even while he prayed for her and her father, he understood how it might be that the man was well content, and how that neither to-day nor to-morrow could he return to that old life of the Priory in the forest.

"Yet," said he, "tell the Prior that surely some day I shall see his face again, if it be but for mere love of him for well I know there be among the monks those who would more joyfully rend me or burn me at the stake than give the hand of fellowship to one who has cast aside the cowl."

When he heard of these things the Prior only prayed the more earnestly for the home-coming of his friend.

Now it was in the autumn of that year, at the season when the days and nights are of one length, that the great inroad of the sea befell. The day had been stormy, with a brackish wind clamouring out of the sea, and as the darkness closed in it was with us as it is with blind men who hear and feel the more keenly because of their blindness and all that we heard was the boom of billows breaking on the long shore and the crying and groaning of the old oaks and high firs in the forest. Then in the midmost of the night we were aroused by so terrible a noise, mingled with shrieking and wailing, that we crowded to the Prior's door. Speedily he rose, and we followed him out of doors, wondering what disaster had happened. The moon was shining brightly; shreds of cloud were flying across the cold sky; the air was full of the taste of salt.

As we gazed about us we saw that the cloisters and the garth and all the space within the walls were crowded with wild birds—sea-fowl and crows, pheasant and blackcock, starlings and thrushes, stonechats and yellow-hammers, and hundreds of small winged creatures cowering for shelter. And when the Prior bade us throw open the monastery gates, out of the sombre gloom of the forest the scared woodlanders came crowding, tame and panting. No one had ever realised that so many strange creatures, in fur and pelt, housed in the green ways. Even the names of many of them we did not know, for we had never set eyes on them before; but among those that were within our knowledge were coneys and hares, stoats and weasels, foxes and badgers, many deer with their does and fawns, and one huge grey creature of savage aspect which we took to be an old wolf.

The Prior ordered that the gates should be left open for any fugitives that might seek refuge, and he went among the wild beasts, calming them with a touch of his hand and blessing them. Then there came a woman, with a child at her bosom and a little lad clinging to her dress, but she was so distracted with fright that she was unable to say what had happened.

When he had given directions for the care of all these strange guests, the Prior climbed up the mound through the tossing trees, and when he had reached the summit he saw to his amazement that the sea had risen in a mighty flood and poured for miles into the forest. The huge oaks and pines of centuries had gone down in thousands, and over their fallen trunks and broken branches the white billows were tumbling and leaping in clouds of spray in the moonlight. Happily the

William Canton

land sloped away to the north, so that unless the wind changed and blew against us the Priory seemed to be in no present danger. Overhead the great cross vibrated in the storm, and the face of the Christ gazed seaward, and the holy arms were opened wide. The sight of that divine figure filled the Prior's heart with peace and confidence. "Whether to live or to die," he murmured, "in Thee, O Lord, have we placed our trust."

Such was the terrible inroad of the sea which broke the western forest of Amounderness. For many a day the land lay in salt swamp till the sands were blown over it and buried the fallen timber; and afterwards the very name of Forest was forgotten, and the people called all that part the Field-lands.

Now it was in this same year that the grievous pestilence named the Black Death raged in England; but it was not till the winter had gone by that it reached Amounderness. Then were seen those terrible days when ships sailed the seas with crews of dead men, and when on land there was burying without sorrow and flight without safety, for though many fled they could not escape the evil, and so many died that the wells of sorrow ran dry. And because of the horror of so many deaths, it was forbidden to toll the bells any longer lest men should go mad. Often no hand could be got for love or for gold to touch the sick or to carry the departed to their graves. When the graveyards were filled, thousands were buried, without a prayer or a last look, in deep trenches salted with quicklime, on the commons or in an open field. Many a street in many a town fell suddenly silent and deserted, and grass grew between the stones of the causeway. Here and there fires were kept burning night and day to purify the air, but this availed little. In many a thorpe and village all the inhabitants were swept away and even robbers and desperate vagrants were too greatly in fear of infection to enter the ownerless houses. Sometimes in the fields one saw little children, and perchance an aged woman, trying to manage a plough or to lead a waggon.

When this trouble fell upon the people the Prior sent out various of the brethren to aid the suffering and to comfort the bereaved; but when many of the monks themselves were stricken down and died within the hour, a great dread took hold of the others, so that they were unwilling to expose themselves to danger.

The Prior rebuked them for their lack of faith and the coldness of their charity. "When the beasts and wild creatures suffered we had compassion on them," he said; "what folly is this that we shall have care for them and yet feel no pity for men and women in their misery! Do you fear that you too may be taken off by this pestilence? Who, then, has told you that you shall not die if only you can escape the pestilence? Daily you pray, 'Thy kingdom come,' and daily you seek that it shall not come to-day."

He went abroad himself unweariedly with one or other of the brethren, doing such good as he was able, and when he had returned home and taken a little rest he set out once more. Now one night as he and Brother Bede returned belated through the forest, they were startled as they approached the gate to hear the weeping and moaning of one who lay forsaken on the cold earth; and when the Prior called out through the darkness, "Be of good cheer, Christian soul, we are coming to your aid," the sufferer replied by rattling the lid of his clap-dish, and at once they knew it was some poor leper who had fallen helpless by the way.

"Patience, brother," said the Prior; and bidding his companion open the wicket, he lifted the wretched outcast from the ground and carried him in his arms into the great

William Canton

hall. "Rest here a little," he said, "till we can bring you light and fire and food."

The Prior and Bede hastened to call the brethren who had charge of these matters, but when they returned with the other monks they found the great hall shining with a wonderful light and filled with a marvellous fragrance of flowers, and on the seat where the leper had been placed there lay a golden rose, but the leper himself had vanished.

Then a great joy cast fear out of the hearts of the brotherhood, and they laboured without ceasing in the stricken villages. Many of them died, but it was without sorrow or repining, and the face of each was touched with the golden rose ere he was laid to his rest.

Now the pestilence of that year was stayed by a bitter winter, and snow lay deep even in the forest, and great blocks of ice littered the shore of the bleak sea. And in the depth of the winter, when it drew near the Nativity, there came riding to the monastery a stranger, who asked to see the Prior. When the Prior looked into the man's face the tears started and ran down his own, and he opened his arms to him, and drew him to his breast and kissed him. For this was indeed the Lost Brother. And when he had thus given him welcome, the Prior said: "I ask no questions; what you can tell me you shall tell when the fitting time comes. But this is your home to have or to leave, for you are as free as the winds of heaven."

And the Lost Brother replied: "Wise are you no less than good. The plague has bereft me of the child, and of the mother of the child. More I cannot tell you now."

Thus to the Priori great happiness the companion of his youth returned from wandering the ways of the world.

When the weeks passed, and still he remained a silent and solitary stranger, the religious spoke sharply among themselves of the presence of one who had broken vows and revelled in the joys of life, and had been received without censure or reproof. Then the Prior, wrathful now even on account of his gentleness, rebuked them once again: "O eyes of stone and hearts of water, are you so slow to learn? Have you who sheltered the wild creatures no thought for this man of much sorrow? Have you who buried the dead no prayer and no tenderness for this soul of the living?"

More than once the Lost Brother seemed to awake from a dream, and spoke of going forth again from this home or quiet, saying: "Truly this is great peace and solace to me, but I am not of you; my thoughts are not your thoughts, nor is yours my way of life. Indeed, though I were to will it never so, I could not repent of what I have done. Let me go; why should I be an offence and a stone of stumbling to those who are righteous among you?"

But the Prior silenced him, asking gently: "Do we distress you with any of these things? God has His times and seasons, and will not be hastened. At least so long as you find peace and rest here, remain with us."

"You are strangely wise and gentle," the Lost Brother answered. "God, I doubt it not, has His times and seasons; but with me I know not at all what He will do."

It was no long while after this that the Prior fell into a grievous illness; and when he knew that his hour was drawing nigh, he besought the monks to bear him up to the foot of the cross on the mound. There, as he looked far abroad into the earth over the tree-tops, he smiled with lightness of heart and said: "If the earth be so beautiful and so sweet, what must the delight of Paradise be?"

And behold! a small brown squirrel came down a tree, and ran across and nestled in the holy man's bosom, and its eyes were full of tears. The Prior stroked and caressed it, and said: "God bless thee, little woodlander, and may the nuts never fail thee!"

Then, gazing up into the blue sky and the deep spaces of air above, he murmured in a low voice, "It is a very awful and lonely way to go!"

"Not so awful for you," replied the companion of his youth. "That blue way has been beaten plain by the Lord Christ, and the Apostles, and many holy men from the beginning."

A long while the Prior lay musing before he spoke again, and then he said: "I remember me of an ancient saying which I had long forgotten. A year for the life of a—nay, I know not what any longer. But after that it runs, And three for the life of a field; and thrice the life of a field for the life of a hound; and thrice the life of a hound for the life of a horse; and thrice the life of a horse for the life of a man; and thrice the life of a man for the life of a stag; and thrice the life of a stag for the life of an ouzel; and thrice the life of an ouzel for the life of an eagle; and thrice the life of an eagle for the life of a salmon; and thrice the life of a salmon for the life of a yew; but the Lord God liveth for ever—the Lord God liveth for ever!"

That same night the alabaster box was broken and the precious ointment poured out. And on the Prior's breast they placed the golden rose, and under the great red hawthorn in the midst of the cloister-garth they laid him, O Lord, beneath the earth which is Thy footstool.

At the same hour in which he was taken from us there was a great crying and lamentation of the wild creatures in the forest, and the tall stags bellowed and clashed their antlers against the gates of the monastery.

In the place of Prior Oswald, Father Bede was made Prior.

Whether the spirit of Prior Oswald ever returned to earth the book does not tell, but the Lost Brother, the companion of his youth, lived in the house of Kilgrimol to old age, and in the days of Bede's rule he made a good end.

William Canton

THE KING ORGULOUS

To and fro in the open cloister of Essalona walked the monk Desiderius, musing and musing. Every now and again he stayed in his paces to feed a tall white stork and two of her young, which stood on the parapet between the pillars of the cloister; and though for the most part his dole went to the storklings, the mother was well content with his stroking of her head and soft white backfeathers.

Then he resumed his slow walk, turning over and over in his perplexed mind the questions of grace and nature, and praying for light in the obscure ways where reason groped darkling. Meanwhile the storks stood grave and patient, as if they too had matter for deep musing.

As in this day, so in the ancient time the convent of Essalona was perched on a beetling crag on the northern side of the Sarras mountains. There the mighty ridge, with its belts of virgin pinewood and its stony knolls and pastoral glens, breaks off suddenly in a precipitous escarpment; and, a thousand feet below, the land is an immense green plain, sweeping away to the blue limits of the north. It is as though the sea had once on a time run up to the mountain wall and torn down the tawny rocks for sand and shingle, and had then drawn back into the north, leaving the good acres to grow green in the sun. Through the plain winds a river, bright and slow; in many places the fruitful level is ruffled with thicket and coppice; and among the far fields the white walls of farms and hamlets glitter amid their boskage. When the clear sunlight fell on that still expanse of quiet earth, one might see, in those days, the stone towers and sparkling pinnacles of the royal city of Sarras, with a soft blue feather of smoke floating over it.

Often had Desiderius let his eyes rest on the smoulder and gleam of that busy city, which was all so hushed and dreamlike in the distance, little thinking the while that one day he should dwell within its walls, and play a strange part in the deeds that men remember.

From the brink of the escarpment rises the rock of Essalona, and the convent is built on the edge of the rock, in such sort that, leaning over the parapet of the open cloister, Desiderius might have dropped a pebble sheer down to the plain below. A single path wound up the rock to the gate, so narrow and steep that one sturdy lay-brother might have held the way with a thresher's flail against a score of men-at-arms.

Here, then, in this solitary house, Desiderius dwelt with five other brethren, all good and faithful men; but he, the youngest and yet the most learned in philosophy and star-lore and the sacred Scriptures and the books of the wise, was the most meek and lowly of heart. No pains did he spare his body or his spirit to master the deep knowledge of divine things. Diligent by day, he eked out the light of the stars with the lamp of the firefly, or conned his page by the dim shining of the glow-worm along the lines.

Now as he mused in the cloister he stopped short with a deep sigh, and stood before the storks, and said: "Away, happy birds; you have leave. Disport yourselves, soaring very high in the sunny heavens, or take your rest on our roofs. I have appeased you with food; but to the hunger of my soul who shall minister?"

At his word the storks flapped their wings and rose from the parapet, and went sailing up into the sunshine; and Desiderius heard at his shoulder a most sweet and gracious voice saying: "What is thy hunger, and wherein wouldst thou have me minister to thee?"

Turning about, Desiderius saw that it was an Angel which spoke, and he fell at the bright spirit's feet, abashed and in great dread. But the Angel raised him up, and gave him courage, saying: "O Desiderius, most dear to me (for I am thine Angel Guardian), do not tremble to tell me; but speak to me even as thou wouldst speak to a man of thy brethren."

Then said Desiderius: "Show to me and make plain, I pray thee, the mystery of the grace of God in the heart of man."

"Many are the mysteries of God," said the Angel, "whereof even the highest of the Archangels may not sustain the splendour, and this is one of them. Howbeit, if thou wilt be patient and prayerful, and wilt repose thy trust in the Lord Christ, I will strive to show thee two pictures of thy very self—one, to wit, of the natural Adam in Desiderius, and one of the man redeemed by the blood shed for thee. So in some wise shalt thou come to some dim light of this mystery of grace divine. Will that suffice thee?"

"That, Lord Angel, will suffice," said the monk, bowing low before the Angel.

"Wait, then, and watch; and even in thy body and before thou diest thou shalt behold as I have said."

Therewith the Angel left him, and Desiderius was aware of

but the walls and pillars of the cloister, and the bright vast plain, and, far away, the city of Sarras glittering, and the smoke sleeping like a small blue cloud above it. And the coming and going of the Angel was after this manner. Desiderius perceived him, bright in the brightness of the sunshine, as one perceives a morsel of clear ice floating in clear water; and when Desiderius saw him no more it was as though the clear ice had melted into the clear water.

Now after the lapse of three short years, and when he was but in his thirtieth summer, Desiderius was summoned from his cell on the lonely mountain, and, despite his tears and supplications and his protestations of ignorance and inexperience and extreme youth, made Archbishop of Sarras. Only one answer was vouchsafed to him. "One of thy vows was entire obedience, and the grace of God is sufficient for thee."

In that same year a horde of the fierce Avars poured out from the round green earth-walls of their mysterious stronghold, which lay beyond Danube, and, crossing the river, fell on Sarras; and clashing with that ravening horde, Astulf the King of Sarras was slain.

Ill had it then fared with the folk of Sarras, city and plain alike, but for a certain Talisso, a free-rider, who from a green knoll had watched the onset. When he saw the slaying of the King, he plunged into the battle, cleaving his way through the ranks of squat and swarthy Avars; and heartening the men of Sarras with his ringing cheer and battle-laughter, shaped them into wedges of sharp iron and drove them home through the knotted wood of their foemen, till the Avars fled hot-foot to Danube water, and through the water, and beyond, and so reached the strait doorways of their earth-bound stronghold, the Hring.

Now, seeing that the King of Sarras had left neither child nor brother to heirship, and that their deliverer was a stalwart champion, young and nobly statured, and handsome and gracious as he was valiant, frank too and open-handed, and that moreover he seemed a man skilled in the mastery of men and in affairs of rule, the fighting men of Sarras thought that no better fortune could befall them than they should choose this Talisso for their king. To Sarras therefore they carried him with them on their merry home-going, and having entered the free town, called the Council of Elders to say yea or nay. With few words the Elders confirmed the choice, and the joy-bells were rung, and great was the rejoicing of all men, gentle and simple, that God had sent them so goodly a man for their ruler and bulwark.

In a week from that the city was dight and decked for the crowning of Talisso. Garlands were hung across the streets; windows and walls were graced with green branches and wreaths of flowers; many-coloured draperies, variegated carpets and webs of silk and velvet hung from parapet and balcony; once more the joy-bells were set aswing, and amid a proud array of nobles and elders and gaily harnessed warriors the new King walked under a canopy of cloth of gold to the High Church.

There in solemn splendour the new Archbishop administered to him the kingly oath, and anointed him with the chrism of consecration, and set the gold of power on his head, and invested him with the mantle of St. Victor and girt about him the Saint's great iron sword set with many jewels on the apple and the cross. As the Archbishop was completing these ordinances, he chanced to look full into the King's face for the first time, and as the King's eyes met his each stood still as stone regarding the other for such a space as it would take one to count four, telling the numbers slowly. Neither spoke, and when they who were nearest looked to learn the cause of the stillness and the stoppage they saw with amazement that the new King and the new Archbishop were as like the one to the other as brothers who are twins. With a slow and audible drawing of the breath the Archbishop took up again the words of the ritual, and neither looked at the other any more at that time.

Now, having been crowned and consecrated, Talisso ascended the steps in front of the altar, and, drawing the huge blade from its sheath, lunged with it four times into the air—once to the north, and once to the south, once to the east and once to the west. Sheathing the sword, he descended, and walking to the western portal mounted his war-horse, and paced slowly down the street, followed by a brilliant cavalcade, to the Mound of Coronation.

Urging his steed up the ascent, he drew rein on the summit, and once more bared the holy brand, and, wheeling to the four quarters of heaven, thrust it into the air in token of lordship and power inalienable; and when he rode down the Mound to his people a great cry was raised in greeting, and four pigeons were loosed. High they flew in circles over-head, and, each choosing his own airt, darted out to the four regions of the world to bear the news of that crowning.

The first years of the new reign seemed to be the dawn of a Golden Age in the land of Sarras, and in those years no man was more beloved and honoured by the King than was Archbishop Desiderius. As time passed by, however, and the evil leaven of unrestrained power began to ferment in the King's heart, and the Archbishop opposed and reproved him, gently and tenderly at first, but ever more gravely and steadfastly, coldness and estrangement divided them; and soon that strange resemblance which gave them the aspect of twin brothers, became a root of suspicion and dread in the King's mind, for he reasoned with himself, "What more likely than that this masterful prelate should dream of wearing the crown, he who so nearly resembles the King that the mother of either might well pause ere she should say which was her son? A foot of iron, and a sprinkling of earth, and farewell Talisso! None would guess it was Desiderius who took his ease in thy chair."

Thus by degrees limitless power waxed into lawlessness, and suspicion and dread into moroseness and cruelty, and on this rank soil the red weeds of lust and hate and bitter pride sprang up and choked all that was sweet and gracious and lovable in the nature of the man.

Then did the wise and gentle folk of Sarras come to perceive how woefully they had been deceived in the tyrant they had crowned, and speedily it came to pass that when they spoke of King Talisso they breathed not his name, but using an ancient word to signify such insane and evil pride as that of Lucifer and the Fallen Angels, they called him the King Orgulous. Yet if this was the mind of the better folk, there was no lack of base and venomous creatures—flatterers, time-servers, and sycophants—to minister to his wickedness and malignity.

Dark were the days which now fell on Sarras, and few were those on which some violence or injustice, some deed of lust or rapacity was not flaunted in the face of heaven. The most noble and best men of the city were attainted and plundered and driven into exile. Of the meaner sort of folk many a poor citizen or rustic toiler went shaven and branded, or maimed of nose and eyelids, or with black stumps seared with pitch and an iron hook for hand. Once more the torture-chamber of the castle rang with the screams of poor wretches stretched on the rack; and the ancient instruments of pain, which had rusted through many a long year of clemency, were once more reddened with the sweat of human agony.

An insatiable lust of cruelty drove the King to a sort of madness. With a fiendish malice he fashioned of wood and iron an engine of torment which bore the likeness of a beautiful woman, but which opened when a spring was pressed, and showed within a hideous array of knives; and these pierced the miserable wight about whom the Image closed her arms. In blasphemous merriment the King called this woman of his making Our Lady of Sorrow, and in mockery of holy things he kept a silver lamp burning constantly before her, and crowned her with flowers.

Now in the hour in which the King was left wholly to his wickedness, he doomed to the Image the young wife of one of the chief men of Sarras. Little more than a girl was she in years; sweet and exceeding lovely; and she still suckled her first babe.

When the tormentors would have haled her to the Image, "Forbear," she said, "there is no need; willingly I go and cheerfully." And with a fearless meekness she walked before them with her little babe in her arms into the chamber of agony.

Coming before the Image with its garland of flowers she knelt down, and prayed to the Virgin Mother of our Lord, and commended her soul and the soul of her dear babe to our Lady and her divine Son; and the babe stretched out its little hands to the Image, cooing and babbling in its innocence.

Then, as though this were a spectacle to make the very stones shriek and to move the timber of the rack and the iron of the axe to human tenderness, the Image stepped down from its pedestal, and lifted up mother and child, and a wondrous light and fragrance filled the stone vault, and the tormentors fled, stricken with a mad terror.

William Canton

Down from the castle and through the streets of the hushed and weeping city the Image led the mother and her babe to their own door, and when they had entered the house, and the people stood by sobbing and praying, the Image burst into flames, and on the spot where it stood there remained a little heap of ashes when that burning was done.

Judge if the land of Sarras was silent after this day of divine interposition. Hastily summoning the Bishops of the realm, and gathering a body of men-at-arms, the Archbishop Desiderius proclaimed from the Jesus altar of the High Church the deposition of the King Orgulous. Talisso was seized and stripped of his royal robes; a width of sackcloth was wrapped about his body, and with a rope round his neck he was led to the Mound of Coronation. There, on the height whereon he had thrust his sword into the four regions of heaven, he received his sentence.

Standing erect in a circle on the top of the Mound the nine Bishops of the realm held each a lighted torch in his hand. In the centre stood Desiderius beside the King deposed, and holding high his torch uttered the anathema which was to sever all bonds of plighted troth and loyalty and service, and to cast him forth from the pale of Holy Church, and to debar him from the common charity of all Christian people. At that moment the Bishops marked with awe the strange resemblance between Desiderius and the King, and the eyes of these two met, and each was aware how marvellously like to himself was the other. But with a clear unfaltering voice the Archbishop cried aloud the doom:

"May he be outcast from the grace of heaven and the gladness of earth. May the stones betray him, and the trees of the forest be leagued against him. In want or in sickness may no hand help him. Accursed may he be in his house and in his fields, in the water of the streams and in the fruits of the earth. Accursed be all things that are his, from the cock that crows to awaken him to the dog that barks to welcome him. May his death be the death of Pilate and of Judas the betrayer. May no earth be laid on the earth that was he. May the light of his life be extinguished thus!"

And the Archbishop cast down his torch and trampled it into blackness; and crying "Amen, amen, amen!" the Bishops threw down their torches and trod them under foot and crushed out every spark of fire.

"Begone," said the Archbishop, "thou art banned and banished. If within three days thy feet be found on the earth of Sarras, thou shalt hang from the nearest tree."

As he spoke the great bell of the High Church began to toll as for one whose spirit has passed away. At the sound Talisso started; then taking the rope from his neck and flinging it on the ground with a mocking laugh, he turned and fled down the Mound and into the green fields that lie to the north.

Not far had he fled into the open country before the reckless-ness of the reiver and strong-thief fell on Talisso. Entering a homestead he smote down the master, and got himself clothing and food and weapons, and seizing a horse, pushed on apace till he came to the red field where he had routed the Avars, and thence onward to Danube water.

Beyond Danube, some days' riding into the north, lay that mysterious stronghold, the Hring, the camp-city of the Avar robber-horde. And thither Talisso was now speeding, for he said to himself: "They are raiders and slayers, and this kind is quick to know a *man*. They will love me none the less that I have stricken and chased them. Rather will they follow me and avenge me, if not for my sake for the sake of the fat

William Canton

fields and rich towns of Sarras."

Now the stronghold was a marvel in the manner of its
contrivance, and in its size and strength; for it was bulwarked
with seven rings, each twenty feet high and twenty feet wide,
and the rings were made of stockades of oak and beech and
pine trunks, filled in with stones and earth, and covered atop
with turf and thick bushes. The distance across the outer ring
was thirty miles, and between each ring and the one within it
there were villages and farms in cry of each other, and each
ring was pierced by narrow gateways well guarded. In the
midst of the innermost ring were the tent of the Chagan or
Great Chief, and the House of the Golden Hoard. Piled high
were the chambers of that house with the enormous treasure
of a century of raiding—silken tissues and royal apparel and
gorgeous arms, great vases and heavy plate of gold and
silver, spoil of jewels and precious stones, leather sacks of
coined money, the bribes and tribute of Greece and Rome,
and I know not what else of rare and costly. Long afterwards,
when the Avars were broken and the Hring thrown down,
that hoard filled fifteen great waggons drawn each by four
oxen.

In the very manner in which Talisso had forecast it, so it fell
out with him at the Hring. The fierce, swart, broad-shoul-
dered dwarfs with the almond eyes and woven pigtails gazed
with glee and admiration on the tall and comely warrior who
had swept them before his sword-edge; and when he spoke
of the rich markets and goodly houses and fruitful land of
Sarras their eyes glistened, and they swore by fire and water
and the four winds to avenge his wrongs.

Little need is there to linger in telling of a swift matter.
Mounted on their nimble and hardy ponies, the Avars dashed
into Sarras land two hundred strong, and tarried neither to
slay nor spoil, but outsped the fleet feet or rumour, till in the

grey glimmer of cock-crow they sighted the towers of Sarras city. Under cover of a wood they rested till the gates were flung wide for the early market folk. Who then but Talisso laughed his fierce and orgulous laugh as he rode at their head and they all hurled through the gates, and, clattering up the empty street, carried the castle out of hand?

Not a blow was struck, no drop of blood reddened iron or stone; and such divinity doth hedge even a wicked king dethroned that when the guards saw the tyrant once more ascending the steps of power they lowered their points and stood at a loss how to act. But Talisso, with some touch of his pristine graciousness, bade no man flee or fear who was willing to return to his allegiance. "First, however, of all things, bring me hither the Archbishop; bring with ropes and horses if need be; but see that not a hair of his head be injured."

Now on this same night that these Hunnish folk were pressing forward to Sarras city Desiderius saw in a dream Talisso standing before the throne of God. On his head he wore his crown, but otherwise he was but such as he stood for sentence on the Mound of Coronation, to wit, with a rope around his neck, and naked save for the fold of sackcloth about his loins.

Beside him stood an Angel, and the Angel was speaking: "All the lusts of the flesh, and all the lusts of the eyes, and all the lusts of the will, and the pride of life this man hath gratified and glutted to surfeiting, yet is he as restless as the sea and as insatiable as the grave. Speak, man, is it not so?"

And Talisso answered, with a peal of orgulous laughter: "Restless as the sea; insatiable as the grave."

"How then, Lord," said the Angel, "shall this man's unrest

William Canton

and hunger be stayed?"

God spoke and said: "Fill his mouth with dust."

Then the Angel took a handful of dust and said to Talisso: "Open thy mouth and eat."

Talisso cried aloud, "I will not eat."

"Open thy mouth," said the Angel sternly.

"My mouth I will not open," replied Talisso.

Thereupon the Angel caught him by the hair, and plucked his head backward till his throat made a knotted white ridge above the neck, and as Talisso opened his mouth, shrieking blasphemies and laughing with frantic rage, the Angel filled it with dust.

Talisso fell backwards, thrusting with his feet and thrashing the ground with his hands; his crown fell from his head and rolled away; his face grew set and white; and then he lay straight and rigid.

"Hast thou filled his mouth?"

"His mouth, Lord, is filled," the Angel answered.

This was the dream of Desiderius.

When citizens came running to the palace, and the Archbishop learned how the gates had been surprised and the castle taken, he lost no time in casting about what he should do. He sent messengers to summon the Council of the Elders, and bade his men-at-arms fall into array. Then he hastened to the High Church, and, after a brief prayer before the altar, girt on the great sword of St. Victor, threw over his purple cassock the white mantle of the Saint, and putting on his head a winged helm of iron, made his way to the castle where Talisso awaited his capture.

"Stay you here," he said to his men-at-arms when they reached the portals, "and if by God's blessing work fall to your hands to do, do it doughtily and with right good will."

Up the high hall of the castle, through the groups of lounging Avars he went, with great strides and eyes burning, to the dais where Talisso sat apart in the royal chair.

"Ha! well met, Lord Archbishop," cried the dethroned King, springing to his feet at the sight of him.

"Well met, Talisso," replied Desiderius in a loud voice. "With no more ado I now tell thee that for thee there is but one end. Thy mouth must be filled with dust."

As he spoke, Desiderius flung back his mantle and drew the holy sword. Heaving it aloft he struck mightily at Talisso. From the King's helmet glanced the keen brand, and descending to the shoulder shore away the plates of iron, and bit the flesh.

Once more the great sword was swung up, for Desiderius neither heard nor heeded the cry and rush of the Avars; but or ever the stroke could fall Desiderius saw the Angel of Essalona by his side and felt his hand restraining the blade; and at the same instant the figure before him, the figure of the King Orgulous, grew dim and hazy, and wavered, and broke like smur blown along a wooded hillside, and vanished from his gaze.

"A little truer stroke," said the Angel, "and thou hadst slain thyself, for of a truth the man thou wast slaying was none other than thyself; as it is, thou art hurt more than need was"—for the shoulder of the Archbishop was bare, and the blood streamed from it.

Bewildered at these words, Desiderius gazed about to see if the high hall and the Avars were but the imagery of a dream. But there in front of him stood the dwarfish tribe, with naked brands and battle-axes. These, when they looked on his face, raised a hoarse cry of terror, for they too had beheld Talisso, how at a blow of the magic sword he had fallen and perished even from the vision of men, and now they saw that he who had slain the King was himself the King. Howling and clamouring, they broke from the hall and fled into the street; and there the men-at-arms did right willingly and doughtily the work which thus came to their hands. Of that fierce and uncouth robber horde, which rode to Sarras two hundred strong, scarce two score saw Danube water again.

When Desiderius knew for a surety that the natural man within him was verily that King wicked and orgulous, and understood that the sins of that evil King were the sins he himself would have committed but for the saving grace of God, a great awe fell upon him, and he was abashed with a grievous dread lest the King Orgulous were not really dead and done with, but were sleeping still, like the Kings of old legend, in some dusky cavern of his nature, ready to awake and break forth with sword and fire. Gladly would he have withdrawn to the solitude of the little convent on the beetling crag, far from the temptations of power and the splendour and tumult of life; but the same answer was given to him now as had been given to him of old: "One of thy vows was entire obedience, and the grace of God is sufficient for thee."

THE JOURNEY OF RHEINFRID

On the green skirts of the Forest of Arden there was a spot which the windings of the Avon stream had almost made into an island, and here in the olden time the half-savage herdsmen of King Ethelred kept vast droves of the royal swine. The sunny loops of the river cut clearings on the east and south and west, but on the north the Forest lay dense and dark and perilous. For in those ancient days wolves still prowled about the wattled folds of the little settlement of Wolverhampton, and Birmingham was only the rude homestead of the Beormingas, a cluster of beehive huts fenced round with a stockade in the depths of the woods.

Among the swineherds of the King there was one named Eoves, and one day, while wandering through the glades of great oaks on this edge of the Forest, he saw three beautiful women who came towards him singing a song more strange and sweet than he had ever heard. He told his fellows, and the story spread far and wide. Some said that the three beautiful women were three goddesses of the old pagan world, and thought Eoves had acted very foolishly in not speaking to them. Others said they might have been the Three Fates, in whose hands are the lives of men, and the joy of their lives, and the sorrow they must endure, and the death which is the end of their days; and they thought that perhaps Eoves had been wise to keep silence.

William Canton

But when the holy Bishop Egwin heard the tale, he visited the place alone, and in the first glimmer of the sunrise, when all wild creatures are tame and the earth is most lovely to look upon, he beheld the three beautiful women, and he saw in a moment that they were the Virgin Mother Mary and two heavenly handmaidens. "And our Lady," he used afterwards to say, "was more white-shining than lilies and more freshly sprung than roses, and the savage forest was filled with the fragrance of Paradise."

Straightway the Bishop sent his woodmen and had the aged oaks felled and the underwood cleared away; and on the spot where the beautiful women had stood a fair church was built for the worship of the true God, and around it clustered the cells of an abbey of Black Monks. In a little while people no longer spoke of the place by its old name, but called it Eovesholme, because of the vision of Eoves.

Now when more than three and a half centuries had gone by, and Agelwyn the Great-hearted was Abbot, there was a Saxon noble, young and dissolute, who had been stricken by the Yellow Plague, and, after three days' sickness, had been abandoned by his friends and followers in what seemed to be his last agony. For the Yellow Plague was a sickness so ghastly and dreadful that men called it the Yellow Death, and fled from it as swiftly as they might. But in the dead and dark of the third night a beautiful Child, crowned with roses and bearing in his hand a rose, had come to the dying thane and said: "Now mayest thou see that the best the world can give—call it by what name thou wilt and prize it at its utmost worth—is nothing more than these: wind and smoke and a dream and a flower. But though all have fled from thee and left thee to die alone in grievous plight, this night thou shalt not die."

Then he was bidden to rise on the morrow—"for strength

shall be given thee," said the Child—and travel with the sun westward till he came to the Abbey of Egwin, and there he must tell the Abbot all that had befallen him.

"And the good Abbot will receive thee among his sons," said the Child; "and after that, in a little while, thou shalt go on a journey, and then again in a little while shalt come to me."

On the morrow Rheinfrid the thane rose from his bed hale and strong, but his whole nature was changed; and he made no more account of life and of all that makes life sweet—as honour and wealth and joy and use and the love of man and woman—than one makes of wind and smoke and a dream and a flower; and all that he greatly desired was to undertake the journey which had been foretold, and to see once more the Child of the Roses.

Westward he rode with the sun and came at nightfall to the Abbey of Eovesholme; and there he told Agelwyn the Abbot the story of his wild life and his sickness and the service that had been laid upon him.

The Abbot embraced him, saying, "Son, welcome art thou to our house, and thy home shall it be till the time comes for thy journey."

For a whole year Rheinfrid was a novice in the house, and when the year had gone by he took the vows. In the presence of the brotherhood he cast himself on the pavement before the high altar, and the pall of the dead was laid over him, and the monks sang the dirge of the dead, for now he was indeed dying to this world. And from his head they cut the long hair, and clothed him in the habit of a monk, and henceforth he was done with all earthly things and was one of themselves.

"Surely, now," he thought, "the time of my journey draws

William Canton

near." But one year and a second and yet a third passed away, and there came to him no call, and he grew wearied with waiting, and weariness begot sullenness and discontent, and he questioned himself: "Was it not a dream of sickness which deceived me? An illusion of pain and darkness? Why should I waste my life within these walls?" But immediately afterwards he was filled with remorse, and confessed his thoughts to the Abbot.

"Have faith and patience, my son," said Agelwyn. "Consider the many years God waited for thee, and grew not impatient with thy delay. When His good time comes thou shalt of a certainty set out on thy journey."

So for a while Rheinfrid ceased to repine, and served faithfully in the Abbey.

In the years which followed, William the Norman came into these parts and harried whole shires on account of the rebels and broken men who haunted the great roads which ran through the Forest. Cheshire and Shropshire, Stafford and Warwick were wasted with fire and sword. And crowds naked and starving—townsmen and churls, men young and old, maidens and aged crones, women with babes in their arms and little ones at their knees—came straggling into Eovesholme, fleeing most sorrowfully from the misery of want.

In the little town they lay, indoors and out, and it was now that the Abbot got himself the name of the Great-hearted. For he gave his monks orders that all should be fed and cared for; and daily from his own table he sent food for thirty wanderers whom he named his guests, and daily in memory of the love of Christ he washed the feet of twelve others, and never shrank from the unhappy lepers among them. But for all his care the people died lamentably from grief and sickness—on no day fewer than five or six between prime and compline; and these poor souls were buried by the brethren. Of the little children that were left to the mothering of the east wind, some were adopted by the canons and priests of the Abbey church, and others by the monks.

In his eagerness to help and solace, the Abbot even sent forth messengers to bring in the fugitives to refuge. Now on a day that Rheinfrid went out on this work of mercy, he met at a crossway a number of peasants fleeing before a dozen Norman men-at-arms. He raised his arm and called to them to make a stand, but they were too much terrified to heed him. Then he saw that one of the soldiers had seized by the hair a fair Saxon woman with a babe at her bosom, and with a great cry he bade him let her go, for his blood was hot within him as he thought of the Saxon woman who had carried him in her arms and suckled him when he was but such a little child. But the Norman only laughed and turned the point of his sword against the monk.

Then awoke the long line of thanes slumbering in wild caves and dark ways of his soul, and with a mighty drive of his fist he struck the man-at-arms between the eyes, so that he fell like a stone. With savage curses the knave's comrades rushed in against the monk, but Rheinfrid caught up the Norman's sword, and with his grip on the hilt of it his old skill in war-craft came back to him, and he carried himself like a thane of the old Sea-wolves, and the joy of battle danced in his eyes.

Ill was it then for those marauders. One of them he clove through the iron cap; the neck of another he severed with a sweep of the bitter blade.

And now that he was fighting he remembered his calling, and with a clear voice he chanted the great psalm of the man who has sinned: "Miserere mei Deus—Have mercy on me, O

William Canton

God, according to Thy loving-kindness; according unto the multitude of Thy tender mercies blot out my transgressions."

The strength of ten was in his body, and verse by verse he laid the Normans low, till of the troop no more than two were left. These were falling back before him as he pressed onward chanting his Miserere, when a body of horsemen rode up and drew rein to watch the issue.

"By the Splendour of God!" cried the leader, as he glanced at the woman and scanned the number of the dead tumbled across the road, "it is a *Man*!"

Rheinfrid looked up at the new comer, and saw a gigantic, ruddy-faced man of forty, clad in chain mail and wearing a circlet of gold about his massive head. At once he felt sure that he was face to face with the Master of England. Still he kept his sword's point raised for another attack, and with a quiet frankness met the Conqueror's imperious gaze.

"Ha, monk! hast thou no fear of me?" cried William, frowning.

"Lord King, hast thou no fear of God?" Rheinfrid retorted.

For a moment the King's haughty eyes blazed with wrath, but William ever loved a strong man and dauntless, and he laughed gaily: "Nay, thou hast slain enough for one day; let us cry truce, and tell me of what house thou comest."

So Rheinfrid spoke to the King about Eovesholme, and the Abbot, and the harbouring of the miserable fugitives, and told the tale of his own fighting that day. And the great Norman was well pleased, and afterwards he gave Agelwyn the custody of Winchcombe Abbey when the abbot of that house fell under his displeasure. As for Rheinfrid he took the woman and her babe into the town; and many others he rescued and succoured, but he neither slew nor smote any man thereafter.

Now for eight long years Rheinfrid lived in the quiet of the cloister, striving to be patient and to await God's own time; and his daily prayer was that of the Psalmist: "How long wilt Thou forget me, O Lord? For ever? How long wilt Thou hide Thy face from me?"

In the ninth year, after long sickness, the soul of Agelwyn passed out of the shadow of this flesh unto the clemency of God, and shortly after his death a weariness of well-doing and a loathing of the dull days of prayer beset Rheinfrid; and voices of the joy of life called to him to strip off his cowl and flee from his living tomb.

As he knelt struggling with the temptation the little Child crowned with roses stood beside him, looking at him with sad reproachful eyes. "Couldst thou not be patient a little while?" he asked.

"A little while!" exclaimed Rheinfrid; "see! twelve, thirteen, long years have gone by, and is that a little while?"

But the Child answered gravely: "An evil thing is impatience with the delays of God, to whom one day is as a thousand years, and a thousand years as one day."

And Rheinfrid knew not what reply to make, and as he hesitated the Child began to fade away. "Do not go, do not go yet," he cried; "grant me at least one prayer—that I shall see thee again at the time I shall have most need of thee."

And the Child smiled and answered: "Thou shalt see me."

William Canton

And the vision disappeared, but the fragrance of the roses lingered long in the little cell.

Then was Walter the Norman made Abbot, and forthwith he began to build a vast and beautiful minster, the fame of which should be rumoured through all the land. Speedily he emptied the five great chests filled with silver which Agelwyn had left, and then there set in a dearth of timber and stone and money, but the Abbot bethought him of a device for escaping from his difficulties. He took into his counsel the wise monks Hereman and Rheinfrid, because they had both travelled through many shires, and he entrusted to them the shrine containing the relics of St. Egwin, and bade them go on a pilgrimage from one rich city to another, making known their need, exhorting the people to charity, and gathering gifts of all kinds for the building of the minster. So with lay-brothers to serve them and a horse to carry the holy shrine, the monks began their journey, and, singing joyful canticles, the brotherhood accompanied them with cross and banners and burning tapers, and set them well on their way beyond the river.

Now think of Rheinfrid and Hereman traversing the wild England of those olden times. One day they were wandering in the depths of the woods; on another they were moving along some neglected Roman road, through swamps and quagmires. Now they were passing hastily through the ruins of some Saxon thorpe which had been burned by the Normans, or lodging for the night as guests at some convent or priory, or crossing a dangerous river-ford, or making a brief stay in a busy town to preach and exhibit the shrine of the saint, so that the diseased and suffering might be touched by the miraculous relics. And all along their journey they gathered the offerings which the people brought them.

"This, surely," thought Rheinfrid, "is the journey appointed me," and his spirit was at last peaceful and contented.

Now in the third week of their pilgrimage they came to a wide moor which they had to cross. A heavy white mist lay on the lonely waste, and they had not gone far among the heath and grey boulders before Rheinfrid, absorbed in prayer, found himself separated from his companions. He called aloud to them by their names, but no one answered him. This way and that he wandered, still crying aloud, and hoping to discover some trace of the faint path which led over the moor. Suddenly he came to the brink of a vast chasm, the depth of which was hidden by the mist. It was a terrible place and he thanked God that he had not come thither in the darkness of the night. As he gazed anxiously on all sides, wondering what he should do next, he perceived through the vapour a tall dark figure. Approaching it, he saw that it was a high stone cross, and he murmured gratefully, "Here I am safe. The foot of Thy cross is an ever-lasting refuge." As he ascended the rough granite steps, he noticed how wonderfully the cross was sculptured, with a vine running up the shaft, and birds and small wild creatures among the vine-leaves, and he was able to read, in the centre, words from a famous old poem which he knew:

Rood is my name; long ago I bore a goodly King;
trembling,
dripping with blood.

As he read them he became aware that some one had come out of the mist and was standing near him. "In the darkness the danger is great," said the stranger; "another step would have carried thee over the brink; and none who have fallen therein have ever returned. But the wind is rising, and this mist will speedily be lifted."

While he was yet speaking a great draught of air drove the

William Canton

mist before it, and shifted and lifted it, and rolled it like carded wool, and in front all was clear, but the light was of an iron-grey transparency, and Rheinfrid saw into the depths of the chasm into which he had well-nigh fallen.

Far down below lay the jagged ridges and ghastly abysses of a gigantic crater, the black walls of which were so steep that it was impossible to climb them. Smoke and steam rose in incessant puffs from the innermost pit of the crater and trailed along the floor and about the rocky spikes and jagged ridges.

Then, as Rheinfrid gazed, his face grew pale, and he turned to the stranger.

"What are these," he asked, "men, or little statues of men, or strangely shaped rocks?"

"They are living men and women," said the stranger.

"They seem as small as images," said Rheinfrid.

"They are very far distant from us," replied the stranger, "although we see them so clearly."

"There seem to be hundreds of them standing in crowds," said Rheinfrid.

"There are thousands and hundreds of thousands," said the stranger.

"And they do not move; they are motionless as stone; they do not even seem to breathe."

"They are waiting," said the stranger.

"Their faces are all turned upward; they are all staring in one way."

"They are watching," said the stranger.

"Why are they watching?" asked Rheinfrid; then looking up into the iron-grey air in the same direction as the faces of the people in the crater; "What huge ball is that hanging in the sky above them?"

"It is a globe of polished stone—the stone adamant, which of all stones is the hardest."

"Why do they gaze at it so steadfastly?"

"Not hard to say," replied the stranger. "Every hundred years a little blue bird passes by, flying between them and the globe, and as it passes it touches the stone with the tip of its wing. On the last day of the hundredth year the people gather and watch with eager eyes all day for the passing of the bird, and while they watch they do not suffer. Now this is the last hour of the last day of the hundredth year, and you see how they gaze."

"But why do they watch to see the bird?"

"Each time the bird passes it touches the stone, and every hundred years it will thus touch it, till the stone be utterly worn away."

"Ten thousand ages, and yet again ten thousand, and it will not have been worn away," said Rheinfrid. "But when it has been worn away, what then?"

"Why, then," said the stranger, "Eternity will be no nearer to its end than it is now. But see! see!"

William Canton

Rheinfrid looked, and beheld a little blue bird flash across the huge ball of glimmering adamant, brush it with the tip of a single feather, and dart onward.

And down in the crater all the faces were turned away again, and the crowd fell into such confusion as an autumn gale makes among the fallen leaves in a spinney; and out of the innermost pit the smoke and steam rose in clouds, till only the jagged ridges were visible; and a long cry of a myriad voices deadened by the deep distance rose like the terrible ghost of a cry from the abyss.

And this was one of the Seven Cries of the World.

For the Seven Cries of the World are these: the Cry of the Blood of Abel, and the Cry of the Deluge of Waters, and the Cry for the First-born of Egypt, and the Cry of the Cities of the Plain, and the Cry of Rachel in Ramah, and the Cry in the darkness of the ninth hour, and, more grievous than any of these, the Cry of the Doom of the Pit.

"Truly," said Rheinfrid, shivering, "one day is as a thousand years in the sight of the Lord."

"Come with me, and I will guide thee from this place," said the stranger. And he led the way along the brink of the gulf till they came to a bridge, high and narrow and fragile, glittering like glass; but when Rheinfrid touched it he perceived it was built of ice, and beneath it ran a fierce river of fire, and they felt the heat of the river on their faces, and the ice of the bridge was dissolving away.

"How shall I pass this without falling?" asked Rheinfrid.

"Follow in my steps," said the stranger, "and all will be well."

He led the way on the slippery ice-work of the bridge, and in great fear and doubt Rheinfrid followed; but when they reached the crown of the arch the stranger threw aside his cloak and spread six mighty wings, and sprang from the bridge to the peak of a high mountain far beyond the burning river. The bridge cracked and swayed, and pieces broke away from the icy parapet.

With a shriek of terror Rheinfrid sank down, and called upon God to help him. Then as he prayed he felt wings growing on his shoulders, and a terrible eager joy and dread possessed him, for he felt the ice of the bridge melting away, and the water of the melting ice was splashing like rain on the river of fire, and as each drop fell a little puff of white steam arose from the place where it fell. So, unable to wait till the wings had grown full, he rose to his feet, and attempted to follow the Angel. But his wings were too weak to bear him, and he fell clinging to the bridge, which shook beneath him.

Once more he prayed; once more his impatience urged him to rise; and once more he fell. And the melted ice rained hissing into the river of fire, and the quick whiffs of white vapour came up from the surface.

Then he committed himself to God's keeping, and waited in meekness and fortitude, saying, "Whether we live or we die we are in Thy charge," and it seemed to him that, so long as it was God's will, it mattered not at all what happened— whether the bridge crumbled away, dissolving like a rainbow in the clouds, or whether his body were engulfed in the torrent of burning.

Then straightway, as he submitted himself thus, his wings grew large and strong, and he felt the power of them lifting him to his feet, and with what seemed no more than the effort of a wish he sprang from narrow way of ice and stood

　　　　　　　William Canton

beside the Angel on the mountain.

"Hadst thou not been twice impatient in the cloister," said the Angel, "thy wings would not have twice failed thee on the bridge. Now, look around and see!"

Who shall tell the loveliness of the land on which Rheinfrid now gazed from the mountain? To breathe the clear shining air was in itself beatitude. He saw angelic figures and heard the singing of angels in the heavenly gardens glittering far below, and he longed to fly down to their blessed company-ionship. Suddenly over the tree-tops of a golden glade he descried a starry globe which shone like chrysoprase, and round and round it a little blue bird flew joyously. And so swiftly it flew that hardly had it gone before it had returned again.

Rheinfrid turned to the Angel to question him, but the Angel, who was aware of his thoughts, said, "Yes, it is the same globe, only we see it now from the other side. Each circle that the bird makes is a hundred years; for five hundred already have you been here, but you must now return."

Then the Angel touched the monk's head, and Rheinfrid closed his eyes, and in an instant it seemed to him as though he were awaking from a long sleep. Cold and rigid were his limbs, and as he tried to sit up each movement made them ache. He found that he had been lying under an aged oak. He rubbed his hands together for warmth, and a white lichen which had overgrown them peeled off in long threads. A heavy white beard, tangled with grey moss, covered his breast, and the hair of his head, white and matted with green tendrils, had grown about his body.

Slowly and painfully he moved from tree to tree till he reached a broad road, and saw before him a bridge, and beyond the river a fair town clustered on the higher ground. So strange a town he had never beheld before—such a town as one sees in a foreign land, built with quaint roofs and gables and curiously coloured. As he crossed the bridge he met a woman who stared at him in amazement. He raised his head to speak, but he had lost the power of utterance. The woman waited; and at last with a feeble stammering speech he asked her the name of the place. She shook her head and said she did not understand his words, and with a look of pity she went on her way.

Then down to the bridge came an urchin, and Rheinfrid repeated his question.

"This is Eovesholme," said the lad.

"That cannot be," said Rheinfrid, "for it is little more than twice seven days since I left Eovesholme, and this place is noway like the place you name."

"Nay, but it is Eovesholme," replied the lad, "and you are one of the monks who used to be here before the King pulled down the Abbey."

"Pulled down the Abbey! Hath King William pulled down the Abbey?" Rheinfrid asked in bewilderment.

"Nay, it is bluff King Hal who has pulled the Abbey down. Come, and you shall see."

The lad took Rheinfrid by the hand and led him through the streets till they came to the ruins. Only one beautiful sculptured arch was left standing, but Rheinfrid had never seen it before. They passed through and stood among a litter of stones, tumbled drums of pillars and fragments of carved mouldings and capitals. Rheinfrid recognised the spot. The

William Canton

land was the same, and the river, and the far hills, but nearly all the forest had been cleared, and the Abbey had vanished. What had happened to him and to them?

"Hast thou where to pass the night, old father?" the lad asked.

Rheinfrid shook his head sorrowfully.

"Then I will show thee a place," he said.

And again he took Rheinfrid by the hand, and let him among the ruins till they came to a flight of stone steps which led down into the crypt of the minster. These they descended, and there was a dim light in the place, and Rheinfrid's heart beat quickly, for he knew the pillars and vaulted roofs and walls of this undercroft.

"Here you may rest peacefully and sleep well," said the urchin; "no one will venture here to disturb your slumber."

"Sorrow be far from thee, little son," said Rheinfrid, speaking he perceived that it was the Child, and that the Child's head was crowned with roses and that he carried a rose in his hand.

Then the aged monk sank on the cold stones of his old minster, faint and happy, for he knew now that he had finished his journey. But the Child touched Rheinfrid's brow with the rose he carried, and the old man fell asleep, and all the crypt was dark.

LIGHTING THE LAMPS

Now that it was the cool of the day (when God walked in Paradise), and the straggling leaves of the limes were swaying in the fresh stream of the breeze, and the book was finished—this very book—and at last, after many busy evenings I was free to do as I pleased, W. V. and I slipped away on a quiet stroll before bedtime.

It was really very late for a little girl—nearly nine o'clock; but when one *is* a little girl a walk between sunset and dark is like a ramble in fairyland; and after the heat of the day the air was sweet and pleasant, and in the west there still lingered a beautiful afterglow.

We went a little way in the direction of the high trees of Caen Wood, where, you know, William the Conqueror had a hunting lodge; and as we passed under the green fringes of the rowans and the birches which overhung the pathway, it was delightful to think that perchance over this very ground on which we were walking the burly Master of England may have galloped in chase of the tall deer.

"He loved them as if he were their father," said W. V., glancing up at me with a laugh. "My history book says that. But it wasn't very nice to kill them if he loved them, was it, father?"

William Canton

We turned down the new road they are making. It runs quite into the fields for some distance, and then goes sharp to the right. A pleasant smell of hay was blowing up the road, and when we reached the angle we saw two old stacks and the beginning of a new one; and the next field had been mown and was dotted with haycocks.

On the half-finished road a steam roller stood, with its tarpaulin drawn over it for the night. In the field, along the wooden fence, some loads of dross had been shot between the haycocks; lengths of sod had been stripped off the soil and thrown in a heap, and planks had been laid down for the wheelbarrows. A rake, which some haymaker had left, stood planted in the ground, teeth uppermost; beside it a labourer's barrow lay overturned. A few yards away a thick elderberry bush was growing dim in the twilight, and its bunches of blossom looked curiously white and spectral.

I think even W. V. felt it strange to see this new road so brusquely invading the ancient fields. I looked across the frank natural acres (as if they were a sort of wild creature), stretching away with their hedgerows and old trees to the blue outline of the hills on the horizon, and wondered how much longer one might see the rose-red of sunset showing through interlaced branches, or dark knots of coppice silhouetted against the grey-green breadths of tranquil twilight.

When we went a little further we caught sight among the trees of some out-buildings of the farm. What a lost, pathetic look they had!

Thinking of the stories in my book, it seemed to me that the scene before me was a figure of the change which took place when the life we know invaded and absorbed the strange mediaeval life which we know no longer, and which it is now so difficult to realise.

Slowly the afterglow faded; when you looked carefully for a star, here and there a little speck of gold could be found in the heavens; the birds were all in their nests, head under wing; white and grey moths were beginning to flutter to and fro.

Suddenly over the fields the sound of church-bells floated to us.

"Is that the Angelus, father?" asked W. V.

"No, dear; I think it must be the ringers practising."

"If it had been the Angelus, would St. Francis have stood still to say the prayer?"

"I think he would have knelt down to say it. That would be more like St. Francis."

"And would William the Conqueror?"

"Why, no; I fancy he would have taken it for the curfew bell."

"They do still ring the curfew bell in some places, don't they, father?"

"Oh yes; in several places; but, of course, they don't cover up their fires."

"I like to hear of those old bells; don't you, father?"

As we reached the end of the new road we saw the man lighting the lamp there; and we watched him going quickly

William Canton

from one post to another, leaving a little flower of fire wherever he stopped. All was very quiet, and, as he went down the street, we could hear the sound of his footsteps growing fainter and fainter in the distance. All our streets, you must know, are lined with trees, trees both in the gardens and on the side-walks, and the lamps glittered among the leaves and branches like so many stars. When we passed under them we noticed how the light tinged the foliage that was nearest with a greenish ash-colour, almost like the undersides of aspen-leaves.

"Isn't it just like a fairy village?" asked W. V.

On our way down our own street I pointed silently to the Forest. High over the billowy outline of the darkened tree-tops the church of the Oak-men was clear against the weather-gleam. W. V. nodded: "I expect all the Oak boys and girls have said, 'God bless this house from thatch to floor,' and gone to bed long ago." Since she heard the story of the Guardians of the Door, that has been her own favourite prayer at bed-time.

Thinking of the lighting of the lamps after she had been safely tucked in, I tried to make her a little song about it. I don't think she will like it as much as she liked the actual lighting of the lamps, but in years to come it may remind her of that delightful spectacle.

THE LAMPLIGHTER

From lamp to lamp, from street to street,
He speeds with faintlier echoing feet,
A pause—a glint of light!
And, lamp by lamp, with stars he marks his round.

So Love, when least of Love we dream,
Comes in the dusk with magic gleam.
A pause—a touch—so slight!
And life with clear celestial lights is crowned.

William Canton

Choose from Thousands of 1stWorldLibrary Classics By

A. M. Barnard
Ada Leverson
Adolphus William Ward
Aesop
Agatha Christie
Alexander Aaronsohn
Alexander Kielland
Alexandre Dumas
Alfred Gatty
Alfred Ollivant
Alice Duer Miller
Alice Turner Curtis
Alice Dunbar
Allen Chapman
Alleyne Ireland
Ambrose Bierce
Amelia E. Barr
Amory H. Bradford
Andrew Lang
Andrew McFarland Davis
Andy Adams
Angela Brazil
Anna Alice Chapin
Anna Sewell
Annie Besant
Annie Hamilton Donnell
Annie Payson Call
Annie Roe Carr
Annonaymous
Anton Chekhov
Archibald Lee Fletcher
Arnold Bennett
Arthur C. Benson
Arthur Conan Doyle
Arthur M. Winfield
Arthur Ransome
Arthur Schnitzler
Arthur Train
Atticus
B.H. Baden-Powell
B. M. Bower
B. C. Chatterjee
Baroness Emmuska Orczy
Baroness Orczy
Basil King
Bayard Taylor
Ben Macomber
Bertha Muzzy Bower
Bjornstjerne Bjornson

Booth Tarkington
Boyd Cable
Bram Stoker
C. Collodi
C. E. Orr
C. M. Ingleby
Carolyn Wells
Catherine Parr Traill
Charles A. Eastman
Charles Amory Beach
Charles Dickens
Charles Dudley Warner
Charles Farrar Browne
Charles Ives
Charles Kingsley
Charles Klein
Charles Hanson Towne
Charles Lathrop Pack
Charles Romyn Dake
Charles Whibley
Charles Willing Beale
Charlotte M. Braeme
Charlotte M. Yonge
Charlotte Perkins Stetson
Clair W. Hayes
Clarence Day Jr.
Clarence E. Mulford
Clemence Housman
Confucius
Coningsby Dawson
Cornelis DeWitt Wilcox
Cyril Burleigh
D. H. Lawrence
Daniel Defoe
David Garnett
Dinah Craik
Don Carlos Janes
Donald Keyhoe
Dorothy Kilner
Dougan Clark
Douglas Fairbanks
E. Nesbit
E. P. Roe
E. Phillips Oppenheim
E. S. Brooks
Earl Barnes
Edgar Rice Burroughs
Edith Van Dyne
Edith Wharton

Edward Everett Hale
Edward J. O'Biren
Edward S. Ellis
Edwin L. Arnold
Eleanor Atkins
Eleanor Hallowell Abbott
Eliot Gregory
Elizabeth Gaskell
Elizabeth McCracken
Elizabeth Von Arnim
Ellem Key
Emerson Hough
Emilie F. Carlen
Emily Bronte
Emily Dickinson
Enid Bagnold
Enilor Macartney Lane
Erasmus W. Jones
Ernie Howard Pie
Ethel May Dell
Ethel Turner
Ethel Watts Mumford
Eugene Sue
Eugenie Foa
Eugene Wood
Eustace Hale Ball
Evelyn Everett-green
Everard Cotes
F. H. Cheley
F. J. Cross
F. Marion Crawford
Fannie E. Newberry
Federick Austin Ogg
Ferdinand Ossendowski
Fergus Hume
Florence A. Kilpatrick
Fremont B. Deering
Francis Bacon
Francis Darwin
Frances Hodgson Burnett
Frances Parkinson Keyes
Frank Gee Patchin
Frank Harris
Frank Jewett Mather
Frank L. Packard
Frank V. Webster
Frederic Stewart Isham
Frederick Trevor Hill
Frederick Winslow Taylor

Friedrich Kerst
Friedrich Nietzsche
Fyodor Dostoyevsky
G.A. Henty
G.K. Chesterton
Gabrielle E. Jackson
Garrett P. Serviss
Gaston Leroux
George A. Warren
George Ade
Geroge Bernard Shaw
George Cary Eggleston
George Durston
George Ebers
George Eliot
George Gissing
George MacDonald
George Meredith
George Orwell
George Sylvester Viereck
George Tucker
George W. Cable
George Wharton James
Gertrude Atherton
Gordon Casserly
Grace E. King
Grace Gallatin
Grace Greenwood
Grant Allen
Guillermo A. Sherwell
Gulielma Zollinger
Gustav Flaubert
H. A. Cody
H. B. Irving
H. C. Bailey
H. G. Wells
H. H. Munro
H. Irving Hancock
H. R. Naylor
H. Rider Haggard
H. W. C. Davis
Haldeman Julius
Hall Caine
Hamilton Wright Mabie
Hans Christian Andersen
Harold Avery
Harold McGrath
Harriet Beecher Stowe
Harry Castlemon
Harry Coghill
Harry Houidini

Hayden Carruth
Helent Hunt Jackson
Helen Nicolay
Hendrik Conscience
Hendy David Thoreau
Henri Barbusse
Henrik Ibsen
Henry Adams
Henry Ford
Henry Frost
Henry James
Henry Jones Ford
Henry Seton Merriman
Henry W Longfellow
Herbert A. Giles
Herbert Carter
Herbert N. Casson
Herman Hesse
Hildegard G. Frey
Homer
Honore De Balzac
Horace B. Day
Horace Walpole
Horatio Alger Jr.
Howard Pyle
Howard R. Garis
Hugh Lofting
Hugh Walpole
Humphry Ward
Ian Maclaren
Inez Haynes Gillmore
Irving Bacheller
Isabel Cecilia Williams
Isabel Hornibrook
Israel Abrahams
Ivan Turgenev
J. G.Austin
J. Henri Fabre
J. M. Barrie
J. M. Walsh
J. Macdonald Oxley
J. R. Miller
J. S. Fletcher
J. S. Knowles
J. Storer Clouston
J. W. Duffield
Jack London
Jacob Abbott
James Allen
James Andrews
James Baldwin

James Branch Cabell
James DeMille
James Joyce
James Lane Allen
James Lane Allen
James Oliver Curwood
James Oppenheim
James Otis
James R. Driscoll
Jane Abbott
Jane Austen
Jane L. Stewart
Janet Aldridge
Jens Peter Jacobsen
Jerome K. Jerome
Jessie Graham Flower
John Buchan
John Burroughs
John Cournos
John F. Kennedy
John Gay
John Glasworthy
John Habberton
John Joy Bell
John Kendrick Bangs
John Milton
John Philip Sousa
John Taintor Foote
Jonas Lauritz Idemil Lie
Jonathan Swift
Joseph A. Altsheler
Joseph Carey
Joseph Conrad
Joseph E. Badger Jr
Joseph Hergesheimer
Joseph Jacobs
Jules Vernes
Julian Hawthrone
Julie A Lippmann
Justin Huntly McCarthy
Kakuzo Okakura
Karle Wilson Baker
Kate Chopin
Kenneth Grahame
Kenneth McGaffey
Kate Langley Bosher
Kate Langley Bosher
Katherine Cecil Thurston
Katherine Stokes
L. A. Abbot
L. T. Meade

L. Frank Baum
Latta Griswold
Laura Dent Crane
Laura Lee Hope
Laurence Housman
Lawrence Beasley
Leo Tolstoy
Leonid Andreyev
Lewis Carroll
Lewis Sperry Chafer
Lilian Bell
Lloyd Osbourne
Louis Hughes
Louis Joseph Vance
Louis Tracy
Louisa May Alcott
Lucy Fitch Perkins
Lucy Maud Montgomery
Luther Benson
Lydia Miller Middleton
Lyndon Orr
M. Corvus
M. H. Adams
Margaret E. Sangster
Margret Howth
Margaret Vandercook
Margaret W. Hungerford
Margret Penrose
Maria Edgeworth
Maria Thompson Daviess
Mariano Azuela
Marion Polk Angellotti
Mark Overton
Mark Twain
Mary Austin
Mary Catherine Crowley
Mary Cole
Mary Hastings Bradley
Mary Roberts Rinehart
Mary Rowlandson
M. Wollstonecraft Shelley
Maud Lindsay
Max Beerbohm
Myra Kelly
Nathaniel Hawthrone
Nicolo Machiavelli
O. F. Walton
Oscar Wilde
Owen Johnson
P.G. Wodehouse
Paul and Mabel Thorne

Paul G. Tomlinson
Paul Severing
Percy Brebner
Percy Keese Fitzhugh
Peter B. Kyne
Plato
Quincy Allen
R. Derby Holmes
R. L. Stevenson
R. S. Ball
Rabindranath Tagore
Rahul Alvares
Ralph Bonehill
Ralph Henry Barbour
Ralph Victor
Ralph Waldo Emmerson
Rene Descartes
Ray Cummings
Rex Beach
Rex E. Beach
Richard Harding Davis
Richard Jefferies
Richard Le Gallienne
Robert Barr
Robert Frost
Robert Gordon Anderson
Robert L. Drake
Robert Lansing
Robert Lynd
Robert Michael Ballantyne
Robert W. Chambers
Rosa Nouchette Carey
Rudyard Kipling
Saint Augustine
Samuel B. Allison
Samuel Hopkins Adams
Sarah Bernhardt
Sarah C. Hallowell
Selma Lagerlof
Sherwood Anderson
Sigmund Freud
Standish O'Grady
Stanley Weyman
Stella Benson
Stella M. Francis
Stephen Crane
Stewart Edward White
Stijn Streuvels
Swami Abhedananda
Swami Parmananda
T. S. Ackland

T. S. Arthur
The Princess Der Ling
Thomas A. Janvier
Thomas A Kempis
Thomas Anderton
Thomas Bailey Aldrich
Thomas Bulfinch
Thomas De Quincey
Thomas Dixon
Thomas H. Huxley
Thomas Hardy
Thomas More
Thornton W. Burgess
U. S. Grant
Upton Sinclair
Valentine Williams
Various Authors
Vaughan Kester
Victor Appleton
Victor G. Durham
Victoria Cross
Virginia Woolf
Wadsworth Camp
Walter Camp
Walter Scott
Washington Irving
Wilbur Lawton
Wilkie Collins
Willa Cather
Willard F. Baker
William Dean Howells
William le Queux
W. Makepeace Thackeray
William W. Walter
William Shakespeare
Winston Churchill
Yei Theodora Ozaki
Yogi Ramacharaka
Young E. Allison
Zane Grey